A Simple Shortcut to Inner Peace & Joy

Living Your True Nature

Also by Julie Sarah Powell

A Story of a Changed Life

A Simple Shortcut to Inner Peace & Joy

Living Your True Nature

Julie Sarah Powell
with Kirsten Gamby BA, MA (Hons), Dip Clin Psych

A Simple Shortcut to Inner Peace & Joy
Living Your True Nature

Published by Julie Sarah Powell, True Nature Centre
1ˢᵗ Edition April 2011

www.TrueNatureCentre.com

Illustrations by Phu M Tran
www.PhuMTran.com

Author Portrait by Rita Newman
www.Newman.at

The information contained in this book is intended to be educational and
not for diagnosis, prescription or treatment of any health disorder
whatsoever. The information should not replace consultation with a
competent healthcare professional. The content of this book is intended to
be used as an addition to a rational and responsible healthcare programme
prescribed by a healthcare professional. The author and publisher are in no
way liable for any misuse of this material.

ISBN
978-0-473-16460-7

This book is written in gratitude to life
for its miraculous beauty.

Thank you, thank you, thank you!

This beauty is who you are; your true nature.
May you live in feeling contact with this essence
from now unto eternity...

Acknowledgements

The intention of this book is to remind billions of people that their spiritual freedom, joy and natural contentment is already here, right now. Thank you to everyone who has helped it blossom into life.

Thank you to Phu for his beautiful artwork, to Elysha for his support and vision, to the market research group for their help and constructive criticism.

With every project like this, there is a whole team of supporters who encourage and assist it to become a reality. You all know who you are, so please receive warm and sincere thanks into your hearts, now!

And thank you to everyone out there who is changing the world by changing their attitude and living the freedom of their heart. We couldn't co-create this planetary transformation without you.

Contents

Chapter Eight *149*

Taking Responsibility for Your Creation

Chapter Nine *159*

More Helpful Hints to Make This Change Easy

Chapter Ten *169*

A Date to Be Finished

Preface
by Kirsten Gamby BA, MA (Hons), Dip Clin Psych

Welcome to *A Simple Shortcut to Inner Peace & Joy: Living Your True Nature*. You have been searching for this all your life, even if you didn't know it.

This manual comes straight from the heart of creation to your heart. The content of *A Simple Shortcut to Inner Peace & Joy: Living Your True Nature* is written by Julie Sarah Powell from the eternal space of the heart. Julie lives in constant and abiding 'oneness' and selflessness, shining a light for us all, not as one to be looked up to and admired, but as one whose only purpose is to give and to show the way to live freely as your true nature. This extraordinary work is the crystallised distillation of many years of experience and practice, which have brought about the dissolution of self in Julie.

This manual contains a powerful means to begin to live in that same self-less, heart-centred way. The writing of this began because Julie was moved to create a program for our group to enable us to help ourselves. This work has grown over time and with the addition of the audio recordings, *A Simple Shortcut to Inner Peace & Joy: Living Your True Nature* has been created.

I searched for information similar to this for forty-five years, but everything good that I found only made me hungrier for more. I had no idea then that I would have the great privilege to take part in the creation of this wonderful work!

A Simple Shortcut to Inner Peace & Joy: Living Your True Nature takes you beyond searching to a solid 'practice' of living your true nature, which can be easily integrated into your life at whatever pace you choose.

This training, of living as the love that you truly are, is one of freedom. No beliefs are needed here; no new beliefs and definitely not any old ones. The beneficial effects of this change of lifestyle are immeasurable, whether you believe in them at the start, or not.

A Simple Shortcut to Inner Peace & Joy: Living Your True Nature provides a clear and simple outline of life as it is; of the constant reflections that life provides for us and how easy it really can be to live in constant union with the heart. From this point, you will begin responding simply and spontaneously to life and be naturally happy.

A Simple Shortcut to Inner Peace & Joy: Living Your True Nature answers all important questions. It makes sense of the whole of life without you needing to look at any of the details.

My role in this manual has mainly been editorial, to help to make some parts easier to take on board for those of you who simply want to be the fullness of heart that you *already* are.

As a clinical psychologist and therapist for twenty years, I have had the privilege to witness hundreds of people change and grow gradually, mainly resulting from the pain in their lives and the need to do something differently. I have also seen this in myself, although I have done my best at times to deny the pain I was in. *A Simple Shortcut to Inner Peace & Joy: Living Your True Nature* will make life a lot easier for all of us. As you will see, pain is simply *not* necessary for growth.

I have noticed in my own life and in that of others, that when people integrate the practice outlined here into their lives, situations no longer stress them in the way they would have previously.

I have also seen that past grief, trauma, long-held resentments and anger resolve naturally, as do long-standing and dysfunctional patterns of behavior, depression, anxiety and many other conditions – without any need for the person to talk about it or look at any of the details.

In therapy, resolution of issues or problems generally takes time and there is sometimes a re-emergence of these issues in another guise. The practice of being the heart takes a person to the core of any issues they have, without the need for analysis. These issues then simply dissolve by diverting attention away from them. This can be likened to a living organism perishing in a vacuum.

This effect then appears to generalise to all aspects of the person's life and if they allow it, they become naturally happy and content in their lives with whatever circumstances are arising for them.

That is what is waiting for you within this life-training manual. You will find the results of many years of research, practice and experience. This closely matches the best parts that have been described in the spiritual traditions through the ages, without any of the difficulties involved. You will cut through to the very core of existence and you will see exactly what you need to do to live in complete freedom in your everyday life.

As you progress through this practical guide, you will experience the feeling of being the powerful peace that you truly are. Your time will not be wasted. You will see right to the heart of the matter, as the secrets of the essence of you are revealed.

Take the fundamental teaching of this book in faith to gain maximum benefit from it. Let this teaching prove itself to you by your fearlessly acting on it and then seeing the results as they flower in your life. If you do this, you will create beautiful change for yourself; anything less is impossible.

For myself life has become wonderfully simple, unfolding beautifully and easefully, even when the appearances would look to others to be difficult. There is less and less fight and drama in life and more simple acceptance of all, just as it is. Along with this there is a contented gratitude for life.

There is no longer a search for something outside or inside of me. My heart is right here, ever and always. Life is a flow of simplicity and all of life naturally points to the heart.

Although from the outside it might look the same as any other to an onlooker, life is now very simple, pleasurable and immensely full. Although life still has its ups and downs I am no longer involved or invested in these. Life simply is. Life is extraordinarily ordinary now.

I will always be grateful to Julie for her patience and determination to walk what she talked and also to all who have walked with us in the heart.

Commit to finishing this book and give yourself a real chance at permanent inner peace and joy, no matter how you feel about it. This teaching has been thoroughly tested by people all over the planet and it works. Take it and run with it as fast as you can!

Introduction

This book and its accompanying audios are a life-retraining system for you to actually be free, happy and all that you can be. It is also a practical manual that contains ground-breaking, pattern-breaking and perspective-altering truth. This is *your* truth and the truth of living your ultimate purpose; living as one with your heart.

A Simple Shortcut to Inner Peace & Joy: Living Your True Nature is the story of you, the revelation of how your heart is always speaking to you through your life and calling you home. It is here for you to open up and to dissolve into this incredible dimension of your true nature. Only you can do this and it *is* entirely possible. As you continue to read further, you will be shown how to listen to this call and how to live in constant touch with this 'one' in your daily life.

The art of life is living the freedom of this 'one' – every day. It involves learning how to live your true nature, in unity with your heart. The art is all about learning to take responsibility for your creation and loving it just as it is. You will learn this art with ease as you progress through this manual.

In making this your primary focus and priority in life, balance will follow, unfolding perfectly and harmoniously. This will ensure that your life is simple and free. This is a love affair that is open to every person on the planet.

This book will reveal to you how important this love affair is to you. From here, it will be up to you to tune in to the pure peace that is true of you and make this the one and only priority in your *every* movement.

Truly, there is nothing else in life that is important. This is something worth imprinting onto your mind forever!

This course is about pursuing the ultimate goal; the goal of living your true nature, as one with the love of your heart! Do your best to let go of your preconceived ideas of how the world works and go beyond what you know. To advance to the next level, you have to let go of the old 'you' and allow a new 'you' to be born; the true 'you.'

The '**you**' in the text of this book is always this true you; the core of you, the very heart of you. This explanation of the word 'you' is necessary because words are hard to use when describing this great matter. Each word carries many images and past mental understandings that the thinking mind layers over the top of what is being shared.

You may think that you understand this book as you read it; and you may. But reading and re-reading it will lead you into a deeper understanding of life and you will come to see more and more deeply into it each time. Reading and re-reading this manual is essential, especially if the thinking mind tells you that you already understand or that you no longer require guidance. As you study every word, you will become more attuned to your heart and more in touch with your real purpose.

Everything that has been shared here is literal and exact. Generally, living from your true nature is made out by the mind to be hard and tiring. The thinking mind may also run the words around in circles. If you are aware of this, you will pay no attention to these thoughts as they arise. Instead, you will live from this one powerful place of peace, fully open and alive.

In most cases, meditation techniques are used to still the mind and assist in bringing peace to your life. Unfortunately, typically the technique brings you to the doorway of your true nature, but doesn't let you in. What is being 'shared' here is beyond meditation. It is the literal stopping of all internal activity and stepping out of the mind and its personal identification. This is a very important difference and distinction to note.

In reality, the instructions in this manual are not to have you doing anything. They are to stop you from what you are already doing over the top of the beauty of life. Through acting on what is being suggested, you will clearly see that the personality, the thinking mind, the feelings and the overall mind are never ever, ever, you. These different aspects will be described in detail to demonstrate this fact.

As you read this manual and listen to the audios, a level of feeling between the words is needed. Do your best to read and listen with the whole matrix of your body's system with openness and surrender. Soon, you will be living your life in this wholesome way.

Although you may not be able to see things at first, each time you read this manual and engage in the practice of stopping and realigning to this moment, and use the audios with focus and diligence, you will come to have a deeply-integrated understanding of who you are and how life really works.

You will notice that some things in this manual are repeated several times. This repetition is essential to help you form the *one* habit of tuning in to the powerful peace that you are and to understand that the *one* lesson in life is constantly being reflected to you.

There are many new ways of looking at life described in *Chapter One*. Therefore, you may need to contemplate and reflect on it slowly to let this new perspective sink in to your system. Please be assured that as you read further into this book, everything will be fully explained. You can also rely on the support audios to help you deeply absorb this new understanding and merge it into your everyday life.

"Reading and re-reading this book will lead you into a deeper understanding of life and you will come to see more and more deeply into it each time."

Look for this symbol to see where the audio program is integrated into this manual. More audio suggestions are also listed in *Appendix Two* and are available from http://www.TrueNatureCentre.com/shortcut-to-inner-peace.

Listening to the audios will multiply the benefits you gain from this program as they will help you to drop below any mental knowledge and into this 'one' that you truly are.

The boxes, such as the one below, contain reminders and calls to take action and to feel into or experience what is being pointed to. Always tune in before you begin with these sections to deepen their impact on you. (Tuning in is described in detail in *Chapter Three*.)

FEEL

In reading and listening to the words, let go of your mind and feel the power of creative inspiration within you that these words so divinely point to.

Feel the words from your direct experience of being tuned in to your heart. Then, you will find that the words will be read straight into the core of your being.

The more you review this manual, the more you will begin to find yourself changing. This transformation will be so natural to you that the further you read, the happier you will become.

Chapters Three and Eight are where you will find the main instructions for establishing and integrating this new habit of tuning in to the powerful peace that you are. In *Chapter Four*, you will learn how to stop and drop the personality package that you have identified yourself as being, and to see and be your true nature. Then, *Chapters Seven and Nine* outline how you can take steps towards building up the time you spend on your relationship with your heart, starting with five minutes and adding any other available time that you possibly can.

Of course, all sections of the book are relevant and are important for you to read and re-read. However, it is also important to make sure that you read the whole manual all the way through at least *three times* before you choose to flip through different areas of it. There is an energetic flow to the book and it is necessary to read from start to finish to experience the full impact of it.

The highlighted quotes are key points that summarise the essence of what is being discussed. These quotes can be focused upon and felt into if you choose. They are also listed at the end of each chapter for an easy at-a-glance review of the key points from that chapter. All of the suggestions in this manual are only being made to help your transition to living your spiritual freedom be easy, rewarding and enjoyable.

When you live from this one powerful place of peace, you will simply start to see that your freedom is actually true and is happening now. You will live clear of the thinking mind and clear of anything that distracts you from your natural happiness, beauty and power.

The only things that you need to bring with you on this path are your openness, focused intent and your willingness to try what is suggested for yourself. This will allow you to have direct, personal and experiential proof of the essence of your true nature. No one can teach you; this material can only guide you to find this true understanding within you. The rest is up to you.

Remember, happiness is a skill that can be learned. This is a new way of being for most people and perhaps for you too.

With abiding openness and focused intent to be as one with your heart, you can only succeed. This unification will transform your life as if by magic. In fact, the transformation is mathematical. It doesn't matter how long this takes; and it needn't take long. What you sow, you will reap. However, you will find that whatever you sow will be multiplied by a fantastic factor. You will be free of the bonds of having to live in a certain way. Instead, you will wake up to living the beauty and joy of a free life, living itself.

You may not realise it yet, but by the time you finish reading this book, you will have learned who you are and why you do whatever it is that you do in your life. You will have also understood how to live in balanced alignment with your true nature.

"No one can teach you; this material can only guide you to find this true understanding within you. The rest is up to you."

As you absorb this information, you will feel deeply in touch with your naturally happy heart. After a while, as you continue to experience living as one with this heart, your life will flower into being everything you have ever wanted.

You have the right to live your spiritual freedom. Take this right and begin without hesitation.

RELAX

Now take a gentle breath and relax.

Make yourself comfortable and settle in to learn about who you truly are.

"The only things that you need to bring with you on this path are your openness, focused intent and your willingness to try what is suggested for yourself. This will allow you to have direct, personal and experiential proof of the essence of your true nature."

What You Have Learnt from the Introduction

Reading and re-reading this book will lead you into a deeper understanding of life and you will come to see more and more deeply into it each time.

No one can teach you; this material can only guide you to find this true understanding within you. The rest is up to you.

The only things that you need to bring with you on this path are your openness, focused intent and your willingness to try what is suggested for yourself. This will allow you to have direct, personal and experiential proof of the essence of your true nature.

Chapter One

Life from Your True Nature

ॐ

Congratulations on having begun living your true nature.

Life from Your True Nature explains the first key to living from your heart; the purest, sweetest, essence of you. This is a guided journey through who you are and how the world works.

In this first chapter you will learn about:

- Who You Are and What is the Heart?

- The Oneness of Life

- The Living World in Your Chest

- Living the Path of True Love

- Joy

- The Essence and Purpose of Life

- You Have Always Been Searching for Your True Nature

- Your Spiritual Freedom

So relax your mind and body as fully as you can, and begin:

Who Are You and What is the Heart?

Let's start at the beginning and describe who you truly are.

You are the one powerful peace that is before, through and beyond creation. Contrary to what you might think, you are not your body or your mind. Your body and mind are the manifested appearance of **you**. **You** are what lies before all of manifestation. This is the truth of you; your true nature.

Whenever **you** is referred to in this book, it is this truth of you and never any of who you think you are (which is usually referred to as the personality package or your creation, but encompasses anything that is not you). The entirety of your creation is not you, it emerges out of you.

Your heart is what emerges from **you** first; it is the source of the life that you see around you. It is the world at its foundation; the sea of potentiality from which everything arises. Through this heart, all of creation unfolds and comes alive. Your heart produces the breath of life itself. It literally blueprints creation.

So you are not your heart and everything comes from **you**. You *are*, even before your own heart. Life (manifestation, creation) begins somewhere and this somewhere is your heart, the pinpointed something that emerges from you first. Your heart pumps life out (the breath of life itself). In your body, your feeling heart can be felt in the centre of your chest. The physical heart is its physical counterpart, pumping life around your body.

This heart of life is here to wake you up and remind you that you are the creator. It does this through reflecting the oneness of life to you in everything you see, feel, touch, taste and hear.

Your creation includes all external life and your inner world of:

- the thinking mind
- feelings
- emotions
- thoughts
- your attention
- your personality

Everything, all of creation, comes from your heart. There is nothing that it doesn't contain. All experiences of life (all external life and your inner world) are the same. They are a creation, which is why telling the difference between the arising experiences and the peace of **you** is so simple.

Your external world reflects this inner world constantly, whether you are able to see it or not. Your external creation includes everything that you can see and feel, everything manifested and everything unmanifested. It includes all of life on this planet and everywhere else, covering all dimensions. It is literally *every* thing.

Any creation is a 'some-thing.' You are the peace that is 'no thing,' which rests beneath creation in this eternal 'now' moment. This is a fundamental truth.

Everything that you desire comes from your heart's desire to live in love, as love. Your heart is happiness; it is all of life just as it is, always, without exception. Your heart is here, embracing and loving you without any need for health, wealth, success, acceptance or achievement.

This love affair with your heart is the only true relationship you will ever have. So, it must be nurtured as you would nurture your most precious loved one. This heart is the compass, the core, the innateness of your beauty. It is the fountain of love that bubbles through your life. It permeates your existence, through everything that you do and feel.

Your heart is the source of the whole of creation. It is the reflection of you within your creation. Again, this heart is not who you truly are. You are the powerful peace that gently rests beneath life, but you have forgotten to live as this 'one.'

There is nothing more that you need to be the core of existence; to be the love that you seek. Irrespective of how your life looks and what reflections you see around you, your heart loves you without conditions. You are already the divinity that is before, through and beyond creation.

To consciously live as the creator that you are, you have to live in unity with your creation; in unity with your heart. Only then will life reflect your true beauty.

Did you understand all this? Read it again and let it sink in – deeply.

All of life is created out of this peace that you are and your heart is the essence of life. You can feel the source of this life in the deepest core of your being. It is the life of you, reflected by the power of your heart.

FEEL

At any moment, you can stop and feel this divinity.

Feel this 'one' powerful peace that you are, now, as it gently rests inside of you.

Whenever there is boxed text as above, it is an invitation to take some time to feel your heart. Then, as you continue to read on, you will learn to feel this as a regular part of your life.

Before moving on to the next section, pause to simply rest and let this new information sink in deeply. It is important to repeatedly revisit this section because it is fundamental. Don't worry if you don't yet understand; simply continue reading as you trust that this is the truth of you and let yourself sink below any thoughts, resting in the powerful peace that you truly are.

"You are the one powerful peace that is before, through and beyond creation."

The Oneness of Life

Your heart is one from which all things are made, filling all spaces and all forms in the universe. It is the energy flowing through all things, like an invisible atmosphere that is so pervasive that it cannot be seen. It just is.

Many studies of quantum physics relating to how the world is made have already shown that there aren't two powers (of the heart and the mind). In fact, there never have been. There is only the 'one' power of life.

Every atom is a reflection of this 'oneness.' Each atom is alive and complete and everything in life is made from these living atoms. Each one of these atoms is obeying the commands of the 'oneness' of life. Therefore, everything in existence reflects your heart, which is 'one' and if you break down any part of life, you will see another reflection of the whole.

The fact that there is only this 'one' means that you are always the only 'one' in the room. Every appearance – your body, all other bodies, the Earth and all of life – is a direct reflection of the essence of you (the 'one' that you are.)

You can say that, in essence, you are always the centre of the universe and every reflection that you see in life is created from the power of this centre. Everything that you see in life is like a hall of mirrors leading to eternity, simply reflecting the beauty of this 'one' that you are.

It may look like there are many bodies, but in reality, there is only one; it is only the peace that you are, which exists.

To clarify: This fact of life doesn't mean the people around you don't exist. This is obviously not the case. However, everyone you see has a very specific function. They are all reflecting the 'oneness' of life to you to help you accept life as it is and love it regardless of appearance.

We are all this 'one.' Every one of us. We are in this together! The appearance of the 'many' is just a reflection of the different aspects or cells that make up the one eternal form. This one form arises out of the essence of your heart and the more you see this 'one,' the more amazing life is.

We can see this one pattern of life in the planet Earth that we live on. This one Earth is made up of billions of different cells. The cells are the people, plants, animals and all of life on Earth. These people, plants, animals and life populate the planet, making the wholeness that we see around us today. Our destiny is for each cell or person that makes up this one form to live in harmony together.

"Your heart is here, embracing and loving you without any need for health, wealth, success, acceptance or achievement."

Your physical heart and your body are also simple reflections of the workings of life. Your body is like a microcosm of the outer world that you see around you. Your one body is made up of billions of different cells. These cells make up the organs. The organs make up the body's different systems. The systems make up the one body.

Without the physical heart pumping life through this one body, none of it would exist.

"This heart is not who you truly are. You are the powerful peace that gently rests beneath life, but you have forgotten to live as this 'one.'"

The Living World in Your Chest

A powerful way of feeling this 'oneness' of life in your body is to imagine the core of this 'oneness' as a little planet Earth that is gently spinning in your chest.

This one planet is the heart of life; the heart of creation. At its centre is the one source of all creation; the essence of who you truly are; the creator of life. This one planet is your feeling heart; the heart of you, out of which all creation and all 'somethings' emerge.

The world is in your chest and every detail of life has been created as a reflection of this gently spinning world.

FEEL

Feel the power of this world in your chest right now.

Feel the source of your creation.

Feel as this presence reveals itself to you.

Feel it shine brighter as you breathe and feel it intensify as you focus into it.

Without judgement or choice, life is simply an exact reflection of what is within you. It is a reflection of the thoughts you listen to, believe and then hold in place. Therefore, the reflection of life on Earth is your creation.

All of life is simply showing you what is within you. All of the details of life as you know it have been created out of the planet Earth that is gently spinning in your chest. This is the truth of life and the reason why life is said to be our greatest teacher.

"The world is in your chest and every detail of life has been created as a reflection of this gently spinning world."

Living the Path of True Love

To live with full responsibility for your creation is a wonderfully free way of life. Do you realise that you don't have to spend your life making a living? We have been doing it wrong all this time.

The tree outside the window doesn't work for a living. All it has to do is relax and it naturally grows. It is given every bit of nourishment and strength that it can ever need, from life. You are loved and nurtured just as much as this tree is. You have simply forgotten how effortless life actually is. And it is all created from this world that is spinning in your chest!

As you live tuned in to the powerful peace that you are, there is no need to do anything that you don't want to do to make a living. Do what you love; whatever is natural to you from the joy of your heart and the reflection of the universe will align in its perfection, just for you.

Would you be surprised to learn that life has always been like this?

Life would be so free and easy if:

- Everyone and everything were treated with responsibility, respect and love.

- Everyone and everything were treated with honest devotion and loyalty.

- Everyone did the natural job that they were born to do from the love of their heart.

IMAGINE

Just imagine what it would be like if every person on the planet was living in full, moment-to-moment contact with this one truth.

Imagine living in one global community, where everyone is automatically accepted and nurtured as the 'one' that you are.

What a wonderful world it would be!

It brings a tear to the eye and an inner glow to the world in your chest just to see it in the mind's eye. Imagine the power of living it! There is no need to imagine it for too long because soon, you will be living as this 'one.' It is already true.

"It may look like there are many bodies, but in reality, there is only one; it is only the peace that you are, which exists."

Joy

When you live the path of true love from the power of this central core, the 'oneness' of existence is deeply felt and this makes life a continual joy. This joy isn't as the mind would think of joy. It doesn't give you a permanent smile on your face. But you will surely be smiling on the inside, regardless of what is happening around you, because a gentle contentment has entered your everyday living.

There can be no discontentment or struggle with any facet of life when you live the powerful peace that you are. When you live as one with your heart, you spread love, naturally and gently, wherever you are and through whatever you happen to be doing. You are the personification of the perfection of the universe.

The way of your true nature is to flow with life. You see without eyes and you feel without hands. You are simply in tune with life, seeing and feeling the life within you and around you in its magnificence and giving thanks in the gentle awareness of this life being a reflection of you.

Forget the job of president, prime minister, or CEO of a giant corporation; you have the most important full-time job on the planet. This job is to relax and live in unity with your heart. As you continue to read this book, you will be shown how to do just this!

To live with your heart, it is not enough that you think about your heart. You must apply yourself to tuning in to its natural rhythm and acting in the way of your true nature in your outward life, by feeling and expressing its beauty and joy. This 'oneness' must be lived. This is the only real success that can ever be achieved.

Your personality is not capable of achieving this success, but you can be it, simply and easily. You can be in harmony with your heart, simply by staying in this moment and paying everyone and everything your full attention. Giving your attention to the words on this page will start the ball rolling, right now.

"When you live as one with your heart, you spread love, naturally and gently, wherever you are and through whatever you happen to be doing. You are the personification of the perfection of the universe."

"This 'oneness' must be lived. This is the only real success that can ever be achieved."

The Essence and Purpose of Life

The universe is eternally aligning especially to show you this truth of life, through every situation, every action and every reaction made by you or anyone else.

The sole purpose of life is to reflect the one lesson. This lesson is that you are already the one powerful peace that rests beneath the reflections of life and that you can relax and live as this 'one' right now.

Living as this 'one' means that you will naturally:

- Be consciously aware in the flow of life

- Be as 'one' with all that you are

- Be the creator that you are

- Nurture your creation; the joy and beauty of life

- Increase, develop, enrich and expand life

Life is to be made use of to this end only. The universe is making all of that effort just for you to see this one lesson. It would be rude of you not to look now, wouldn't it?

Until you learn this one lesson, you will continue to be faced with this lesson repeatedly – from every angle. What's more, the universe makes the lesson louder with each attempt to help you learn it.

Your heart's design is to teach you this lesson. Understanding this fact allows the natural happiness of your heart to reach into your system and to flow into your daily living. This enables you to see that the 'oneness' of life is actually true and is happening right through you already.

This purpose of life guides you to live to your highest potential and wants you to have all that you can, or will, use for the living of the most abundant life.

When you align with the powerful peace that you truly are, the divine plan for your existence is then free to bring balance to your everyday living. Do remember that freedom is not the goal. You are already free. Living this freedom in your everyday life is what you are here to learn!

"You can be in harmony with your heart, simply by staying in this moment and paying everyone and everything your full attention."

You Have Always Been Searching for Your True Nature

As mentioned earlier, your heart is the essence of creation. You are the creator and your heart is the core of your creation.

Do you really feel that the creator would make it hard for itself to live the love of its creation?

Of course not!

A natural and overwhelming love of your true nature (truth, reality, God, being, your heart or whatever you wish to call it) is hard-wired into every person on the planet, to draw you back into the 'oneness' of life. This love is beyond the dimension of your personality and as you will see shortly, this love is always here and you can tune in to it whenever you like.

This love is what urges you to search for the natural happiness of your heart, to begin with. This love is also what causes a heartfelt response to the pure beauty of life, such as nature; a newborn baby or animal; and words or music that express a reflection of this purity and 'oneness.'

Deep within you, you are always searching for your true nature because you are aware that it is the key that will unlock your life. You were born with this love for who you truly are. It is the hole in your being that you constantly try to fill; the longing for love that you feel with every fibre of your being.

Unfortunately, you have forgotten the love and 'oneness' of life and you look for your true nature in the reflections of life instead of within yourself.

You look for your heart in others; wanting to be:

- loved

- praised

- acknowledged

- appreciated

You would like a partner to give you this; and also your parents, your children and friends to give you this. It is from these people in your life that you receive hints of this longed-for love, reflections of the potential of life. Somehow, though, it is never quite right and never enough.

"The sole purpose of life is to reflect the one lesson. This lesson is that you are already the one powerful peace that rests beneath the reflections of life and that you can relax and live as this 'one' right now."

You can feel there is fullness and depth to life. If only you could continually tap into it! Happiness seems to escape you. It is always just out of your grasp, hiding around the next corner. The grass is always greener on the other side. However, when you get over to that side, somehow the grass is still greener on the other side.

You look for the happiness of your true nature in external things such as food, coffee, alcohol and drugs. From these, you get hints of pleasure and instant hits of temporary gratification.

Drugs might have even shown you a glimpse of what you have been looking for, but taking more of these drugs hasn't worked. The more you consume them, the more you need to take them. The long-term price you pay is very high for this short-term idea of pleasure. Moreover, it does not and cannot deliver the everlasting peace and joy that you know is yours; this everlasting peace and joy, which you feel has just been misplaced somewhere along the line.

You also look for your true nature in money and what money can buy – clothes, cars, houses, security. But, if you ever have these material possessions, there is still something missing. You still want more.

What is it that you want? What is it that you truly long for that lies beneath this external stuff? God? Maybe you've gone to church for years. Or maybe you've taken another spiritual path. You might have caught glimpses of God and felt moments of magnificent splendour.

REMEMBER

Do you remember how it felt to have these experiences of God?

Recall how it felt to feel the light of love shining on your face and in your chest, even for a brief instant.

That is your heart calling you home. This is the experience of a moment of truth. Without living the 'oneness' of life, you can only catch glimpses and experiences of happiness and only feel the purity of its ordinary beauty for moments. And because you feel it only for these short moments, it seems extraordinary.

This hole in your life cannot be filled by either internal or external possessions or experiences. Only staying tuned in to the true beauty and 'oneness' with your heart can bring lasting peace, healing and contentment to your life.

"Deep within you, you are always searching for your true nature because you are aware that it is the key that will unlock your life."

Your Spiritual Freedom

It is vital to realise that only the thinking mind possesses knowledge. Your true essence doesn't need knowledge; it just is.

There are too many distractions when you listen to the thinking mind. As a result, you hardly ever get to truly experience living as this 'one.' You must stop listening to it! You must!

You know it is important to break the pattern of the addiction of listening to the mind. Just look at the impact it has on your life and how it makes you feel when you are lost in its chattering. You may think "A little thought isn't going to hurt me". How wrong can you be? That one little thought begins the momentum of the thinking mind and its incessant thought streams, rather than deliberately creating the space that will bring you to freedom.

LOOK

Look now and see the bad decisions, grief and pain the thinking mind has brought you; the mistrust, doubt, fear and destruction.

See how miserable and full of regret you will be if you continue to be stuck exactly where you are now.

Now, step out of that feeling and see that it is totally unnecessary. Tune in and relax into peace.

Breathe in that peace and support from life and breathe out any anxiety from your system.

And relax!

FEEL

Feel the perfection and happiness that is here.

Feel the relief of dropping the heaviness of the thinking mind and the lightness of just being here; present in this moment.

Ahhhh...

Remember that the thinking mind is a 'something.' It arises from you. It is not and never can *be* you.

This motion of listening to the thinking mind and its ideas of knowledge is the one and only thing that stops you from living the fullness of your true nature. In *Chapter Three* we will explain how to easily tune in to living in harmony with your heart and you will find that this one simple motion will change your life forever.

Your heart is the spark of power that causes the explosion of life. The deeper you delve into it, the more dynamic your life becomes.

When you form the clear intention to stay tuned in to your true nature and you tune in with faith and purpose as often as you are able to each day, you will relax deeper and deeper into living as this 'one' that you are.

Your true essence is the source of life, which is always resting beneath the thinking mind and the idea of your personality. It is absolutely wonderful to live from this natural place of freedom. Living as this 'one,' you will move from being competitive to being creative. From this source of life, there is never any competition. Who would you compete with?

The powerful peace that you are is entirely unknown to the thinking mind. It is the untouchable essence that remains constant throughout all change.

REMEMBER

Allow yourself to drift back to when you were a small child.

Do you remember how you felt in the core of your being?

That's right, the body has changed but the essence of you that you felt ten, twenty or thirty years ago is the essence that you feel today and will feel tomorrow. This essence is beyond the understanding of the thinking mind. It simply cannot be understood, it can only be lived.

> "This motion of listening to the thinking mind and its ideas of knowledge is the one and only thing that stops you from living the fullness of your true nature."

You will already have had flashes of what it feels like to be as one with your heart every now and then throughout your life. These flashes of truth are like a breath of air to a drowning man.

These moments, where the truth is glimpsed and known on a deep level, make life worth it through all of the hard times. They are moments when the beauty and potential of life is seen and you feel natural joy and inspiration shining from the spinning planet in your chest and flooding through your body.

You can feel the motion of your true nature by the open embrace and empty surrender to life and the acceptance of everything as it is.

As you feel this motion, you will start to feel increasingly better about yourself and your life. You will feel that you are free from personally identifying with your creation and completely free from your personality in its entirety.

The creations of life (all external life and your inner world of the thinking mind, feelings, emotions, thoughts, your attention, personal identification) are certainly not the peace that you are. The origin of your inner world, as you presently know it, is personal identification with the thinking mind. The outer world is nothing more than a reflection of this inner world. This will be discussed in depth a little later.

The purpose of any creations of life is solely to show you the one lesson; that you are already this 'one.' So, to be truly free to learn this lesson and live as this 'one' that you are, you need to re-program the way you automatically live your life.

It only takes a short time of re-programming before your automatic move is to stay here as your true nature, instead of automatically choosing to act out your personality and its feeling of separation from your true essence.

Just as it is for the whole of creation, living the powerful peace that you are is completely mathematical.

Choosing 1 moment of freedom + 1 moment of freedom = 2 moments of freedom.

However, before you know it, the numbers are building and building until you are living your natural freedom in each moment of your life in the full understanding that you are already one with this life.

> **"Remember that the thinking mind is a 'something.' It arises from you. It is not and never can *be* you."**

You will also come to understand that there is only one moment to live in: the present moment.

Are you ready to accept the challenge and live as this 'one'?

It will only take a moment to truly break through to your natural happiness; this eternal moment of now. Simply continue reading and you will find that this breakthrough will happen. You are already the 'one' you have been waiting for. Therefore, you *will* stabilise as this 'one.' It truly *is* your destiny.

> **"When you form the clear intention to stay tuned in to your true nature and you tune in with faith and purpose as often as you are able to each day, you will relax deeper and deeper into living as this 'one' that you are."**

What You Have Learnt from Chapter One

You are the one powerful peace that is before, through and beyond creation.

Your heart is here, embracing and loving you without any need for health, wealth, success, acceptance or achievement.

This heart is not who you truly are. You are the powerful peace that gently rests beneath life, but you have forgotten to live as this 'one.'

It may look like there are many bodies, but in reality, there is only one; it is only the peace that you are, which exists.

The world is in your chest and every detail of life has been created as a reflection of this gently spinning world.

When you live as one with your heart, you spread love, naturally and gently, wherever you are and through whatever you happen to be doing. You are the personification of the perfection of the universe.

This 'oneness' must be lived. This is the only real success that can ever be achieved.

You can be in harmony with your heart, simply by staying in this moment and paying everyone and everything your full attention.

The sole purpose of life is to reflect the one lesson. This lesson is that you are already the one powerful peace that rests beneath the reflections of life and that you can relax and live as this 'one' right now.

Deep within you, you are always searching for your true nature because you are aware that it is the key that will unlock your life.

This motion of listening to the thinking mind and its ideas of knowledge is the one and only thing that stops you from living the fullness of your true nature.

Remember that the thinking mind is a 'something.' It arises from you. It is not and never can *be* you.

When you form the clear intention to stay tuned in to your true nature and you tune in with faith and purpose as often as you are able to each day, you will relax deeper and deeper into living as this 'one' that you are.

Chapter Two

Life as You Know It and The Principle of Personal Identification

ℰ

Here we are going to build on the previous chapter and you will find much of the information repeated or in different words. You will also be given many useful new ways to look at the thinking mind and personal identification. These analogies will help you let go of your identification with the thinking mind, the body and the personality. Again, read with openness and trust that you will be guided more deeply into your heart as you progress through.

In **Life as You Know It and The Principle of Personal Identification** you will learn about:

- How Everyday Living Is Based on Belief in the Thinking Mind

- The Shallowness of the Personality

- Underneath the Appearances of Life

- Principle of Personal Identification – What's it Got to Do with My Trousers?

- The Thinking Mind and the Personality Package

- Your Body

- The Thinking Mind is in Overdrive

- Stop Listening to the Thinking Mind

This chapter is longer than the last one, so remember to take it slowly and let it all sink in. Now it is time to read, rest in your heart and enjoy!

Everyday Living Is Based on Belief in the Thinking Mind

This chapter will show you some background facts about life as you know it and how this life really operates. Parts of this may be a little hard to accept. However, faith and acceptance of this new perspective will bring ease to living your true nature.

The next chapter will then show you how to tune in to your true nature and how to live as this 'one.' It's time to suspend any beliefs you have and to read on with an open heart.

Just to recap on what you have learnt so far, let's repeat those core points again:

- There is only 'one.'

- In its essence, life is the one original arising that is formed out of the silence that is before creation; the powerful peace that you are.

- This life is a reflection of the one heart that is within you; the heart of your creation and the reflection of your essence within creation.

- There is one lesson to learn through this life; the lesson that you are already the one powerful peace that rests beneath the reflections of life and you can relax and melt into living as this 'one' right now.

- There is one habit that you have continued to play out; the habit of forgetting that you are this 'one.' Instead, you have believed that you are the thinking mind and a personality package.

So, now that these facts are clear, you can see that life as you know it is not lived from your true nature; from the essence of love that you truly are. At this point, your everyday life is lived as if you are separate from this love, with no real purpose or power.

Can you see this?

LOOK

Take a moment now to feel your motion in life.

Do you feel as one with all others in the free flow of giving and receiving or do you feel separate in your own little world?

Up until now, your life has been based on the original belief that you hold onto, of this idea of the package of your personality that you know as me, myself and I. Your personality is a single package, one complete stand-alone unit. It is another reflection of the 'oneness' of life.

There are billions of different thoughts, ideas and beliefs that make up this one package. These thoughts make up ideas. The ideas then constitute your personality's beliefs. And without you mistaking it all to be who you truly are, none of it would exist.

"You *will* stabilise as this 'one.' It truly *is* your destiny."

The origin of the thoughts that create the ideas and beliefs are the waves of mental activity that are produced by your brain. Over time, these waves have become unbalanced and the left hemisphere of the brain has taken the driving seat. This has created the thinking mind and the endless tapes that run through it.

The one motion of personally identifying with the personality is based in the left hemisphere of the brain. Tuning in to your heart corrects this imbalance and brings the right hemisphere of the brain back into its natural equilibrium.

This creation of the unbalanced brain function and its fragmented personality acts as a filter through which you see and experience your life. This filter creates your personal philosophy of life; the do's and don'ts and the shoulds and shouldn'ts. These fragments and filters cause inner conflict through their contradictions.

With time, the left-hemisphere-based thinking mind has separated this one package into varied expressions. These expressions are the different character traits that the mind judges as good or bad, right or wrong and fixed or broken.

The mind-made personality package includes all of the characteristics of your sense of self. This includes, but is not limited to, your:

- conscious-self
- unconscious-self
- ego-self
- feeling-self
- higher-self
- lower-self
- little-self
- true-self
- knowing-self

It also includes all characteristics of the body, such as:

- mind-body
- inner-body

42

- pain-body

- physical-body

- astral-body

- feelings

- emotions

- time

- and every other incorrect idea and personal belief that the thinking mind uses to separate you from your heart.

Everything that happens within this person that you have believed yourself to be is completely mixed with personal identification. So, initially, it may be hard to see that the thinking mind, feelings, emotions, thoughts and your attention are not who you truly are.

Deep down, you already know that the essence of you is free from these things. However, this one habit of personally identifying with the thinking mind and its ideas leads to the creation of this person and to the selfish behaviour that keeps your identification as the person alive. This isn't something to feel guilty about. It is just a fact through which you have to see, accept and learn the one lesson of life.

The fundamental nature of life is that it is simply thoughts and ideas that you perceive to have form. Any creation of life cannot be the 'one' that you are; it merely arises out of this powerful peace as a reflection of this peace. Therefore, any idea can be dropped in the blink of an eye because it is simply your creation.

It is only when you embrace the idea that the personality package is who you are and you personally identify with these different expressions of the personality, that pain and suffering is created.

You have believed yourself to be this flimsy idea of your personality for a very long time. However, this belief is just a big fat lie! The package of the personality is not a problem to be 'fixed.' There is nothing broken, so there is nothing to fix. There are no problems with your personality being just as it is. Your personality is perfectly fine.

"Up until now, your life has been based on the original belief that you hold onto, of this idea of the package of your personality that you know as me, myself and I."

> "This one habit, of personally identifying with the thinking mind and its ideas leads to the creation of this person and to the selfish behaviour that keeps your identification as the person alive."

This may seem difficult to understand but it is not the personality that is problematic. It is only your thinking mind's judgement of it and your identification with it as being who you are that causes you any distress.

You are not called to judge your personality or attempt to change it. You just need to step outside of the identification with this person that you think you are and see the person as it is. You are called to simply see it, without fear or favour. This involves bringing your attention back inside your body and feeling the 'oneness' that is here, through tuning in to your true nature.

You will then face the good, bad and ugly parts of your personality and your life, without wanting to change them. You will take responsibility for your creations, by accepting them, allowing them to just be here, and naturally relaxing your grip on them.

Acceptance, allowing and naturally letting go occur when you are tuned in and resting in the powerful peace that you are. This opens up the door to change. Wanting change only blocks any change from happening because this wanting is always from the thinking mind and never from the natural happiness of your heart. Your true nature is always happy with life being just as it is, regardless of the appearance of any circumstances that you find yourself in.

Seeing how you personally identify with the ideas of the thinking mind is in itself a recognition that the personality is not who you are. Seeing the motion of the mind shows you that personally identifying with what it says is neither true, nor necessary.

> "You are not called to judge your personality or attempt to change it. You just need to step outside of the identification with this person that you think you are and see the person as it is."

The Shallowness of the Personality

The distortion created by the thinking mind's idea of the personality leads to selfish, immature and self-gratifying behaviour. This behaviour has many hidden agendas and unknown motivations that are unconsciously acted out all through your life. Owing to this, the beauty and joy of selfless living and giving has been temporarily forgotten.

This idea of the personality acts like a layer of film, which gently covers over the powerful peace and natural happiness that you are. This layer of film also acts as a magnifying glass. This magnifying glass falsifies everything that happens in the mind and everything that happens in your life. The magnification exaggerates the details of life and makes these details seem much larger and more important than they truly are. Again, the details are a simple reflection of the 'oneness' of life and can help you to learn the 'one' lesson. All of creation is here to remind you that you are one with this life and you can live as this 'one,' now.

Regardless of the apparent depth in your personality and how this personal identification has been built up through your life, your personality is an entirely shallow and superficial motion. Your personality is not just shallow and superficial in its outward projection, although this is also true, but it is actually and only shallow and superficial.

You perform this personality. It is literally as if you are an actor reading lines and you have become embroiled in believing these lines as being what you truly think and feel. It is only when you look deeper than this acting into what is underneath the play that you are performing in, you will see the limitless beauty and peace over which you perform.

"Acceptance, allowing and naturally letting go occur when you are tuned in and resting in the powerful peace that you are. This opens up the door to change."

Underneath the Appearances of Life

As you live from this 'one' that you are, you will realise that your true essence is already finished and that no idea from the thinking mind is ever able to touch it, regardless of any appearances and ideas to the contrary.

How life looks is just what is on the surface. The real details of life are never how the thinking mind presents them to you. Never look at the appearance of life as being true!

The appearance is like a mist that can be seen through, although you have to look a little more deeply to see what is really here. As you live tuned in to your true nature, you will always focus your attention to what lies beneath the appearance of life and see the limitless depth and riches that are hidden there. To believe the appearances and listen to the thinking mind as it regurgitates the same stories is easy. To look past the appearances and see the truth takes effort, although this effort is only needed at the beginning.

"You perform this personality. It is literally as if you are an actor reading lines and you have become embroiled in believing these lines as being what you truly think and feel."

Then, before long, you will learn to approach situations in a calm and fearless way because you will know that the appearance of life is never as the thinking mind projects. You will also only use the details of the feelings, thoughts, ideas and beliefs to see what is going on within the personality and within the mind, as a reflection of what you hold within you.

Regardless of the appearance, the road of life is encrusted with diamonds and jewels, all showing you the one simple lesson. These diamonds and jewels will be seen as you live as one with your heart and you begin to see and feel deeper than the surface details. This deeper understanding of how life works will bring many insights into the hidden agendas and motivations contained in the personality. These insights will show you how superficial and weak the personality truly is.

Again, it is not the personality that is problematic, but your identification with it as being you. This deep understanding develops real maturity, inner strength and spiritual freedom.

As you stay tuned in to your true nature, you will find that none of the ideas that you hold on to are real and they can never touch this 'one' that you truly are. You also see that life is teaching you to live as this 'one' with every possible sign and motion that it can provide.

As you witness this, your vision of life will grow. You will become more aware of the gap between the distorted and deceptive appearances created by the thinking mind and the truth of things just as they are. You will see your entire life in a new light; in the light of your heart.

"As you live tuned in to your true nature, you will always focus your attention to what lies beneath the appearance of life and see the limitless depth and riches that are hidden there."

Principle of Personal Identification – What's it Got to Do with My Trousers?

> ### IMAGINE
>
> Imagine, for a moment, your favourite pair of trousers.

You know that you have this pair of trousers; you know what colour they are, what size or fit they are and when you wear them they feel almost as if they are a natural part of your body. You become more unconscious of these trousers, the longer you have them on. When you wear these trousers, you don't even feel them most of the time. They are just what you are wearing as you immerse yourself in the day's activities.

However, because you change your clothes at the end of the day, it reminds you and makes you aware of the fact that you are not these trousers. It reminds you that you just *have* trousers.

Your personal identification with your personality is similar to your trousers, except that there has been no reminder to take them off and you have forgotten that it's not you. Now this is your reminder!

It is well and truly time to take the personality off and give it a good wash in the 'oneness' of your heart.

The Thinking Mind and the Personality Package

Delving slightly deeper into this, to the thinking mind and the personality package (or ego as it is commonly known), you can see that they also fall into the same law of not being who you are, just like your trousers.

This thinking mind is every one of the unconscious thoughts that you instantly believe to be true, without looking into whether they are really true or not. These mistaken ideas that you have carried around are totally understandable, because, since just after birth, you haven't known life any other way. But the thinking mind is not you; it is simply a tool that is at your disposal to use.

This can be hard to see at first because the thinking mind has created the personality package, which has been your constant companion for as long as you can remember. Moreover, there has been no daily reminder provided to take it off and help you see that it is not you.

The only thing that keeps this idea of the personality alive is you! You believe in the thinking mind's creation of the personality and then you bring it into this moment as if it is real and you act it out all through your life. However, in reality, your personality is just a flimsy idea that the thinking mind conjured one day.

The idea of the personality was taken on little by little, until it took root in the consciousness of humanity. The thinking mind and its idea of personal identification has been passed on from generation to generation ever since.

"The thinking mind is not you; it is simply a tool that is at your disposal to use."

This fact, that the personality package is not who you are, has been forgotten for so long and the personality package has been identified with for such a long period of time, that it looks and feels as if this personality truly is you.

Now that your personality has been personally identified with to such an extreme degree, when you look at the personality it looks incredibly deep, mysterious and all-encompassing, with no possible way out of it. It feels as if you can just see the tip of the giant iceberg of your personality because it looks so unbelievably huge. It also feels as if this personality is a complex maze of tangled issues, which you need to sort through and untangle before you are ready and able to drop the issues and find your way out of the maze to freedom.

It may even make you believe that each issue is somehow glued to you and needs to be looked into deeply and only then will you feel ready to let the issue go. This is simply not true! As you read on, you will be shown quite clearly why it is safe to drop and let go of all of these issues. You will see that there is really only one issue to drop and that is personal identification with the thinking mind.

Initially, you may not be able to make a distinction between you and this personality package, but here is a clue.

You will clearly see and feel the motion of this idea of your personality when you feel:

- close-fisted

- confused

- superior

- inferior

- dramatic

- complex and problematic

- a knot in the gut

- you know it all

- dissatisfied with life

- the drive to move outward to gain from life

- a staunch refusal to let go and surrender to life

- pig-headed

As you see and feel this, you see that your personality is not actually who you are and therefore, that none of this is any problem at all. Seeing your personality in this way reminds you that it is not you.

Remember that your heart is the one and only power there is and that power is created by you. The power is in the pure potentiality that rests in the peace and stillness of the void within and is reflected to you by life. This shows that the thinking mind has no power of its own. The only power that the mind has is when you give it the one power of your heart, through your attention.

When you tune in and live as one with your heart, you realise this and are immediately released from the mind's influence. From this place of freedom, you will see that there is no such thing as the thinking mind's superficial ideas of the personality or personal identification and you will easily drop these false ideas.

It is this gift of awareness that is alive in every one of us; this connection to the true love of existence. This connection is here for you when you tune in and relax into the powerful peace that you are.

You might well ask, "What does the mind think it's playing at, to try to change the true source of life?" Obviously it can't, so don't even let it bother trying!

The mind cannot see the heart because the heart is everything; there is nothing outside of it to observe it. The mind is simply a cog in the mechanism of your heart, so the thinking mind cannot guide you to it. The mind cannot see itself either. However from the heart, the mind and its workings can be seen. You also cannot see your heart. But you can feel it right now when you tune in, relax and melt into it.

You would be correct every time if, with each idea that came from the thinking mind, you said "That is untrue." Even if life appears to move in the same direction as that thought or idea, in the moment of thinking it, it was actually *not* true. Seeing the thinking mind in this way reminds you that you are not the thinking mind.

"The power is in the pure potentiality that rests in the peace and stillness of the void within and is reflected to you by life. The only power that the mind has is when you give it the one power of your heart, through your attention."

Your Body

Are you beginning to see how this principle works now?

49

"You would be correct every time if, with each idea that came from the thinking mind, you said "That is untrue." Even if life appears to move in the same direction as that thought or idea, in the moment of thinking it, it was actually not true."

Just to be sure, investigate slightly deeper with this principle of personal identification. Look at the body and you can see that the same law applies.

You already know that you have a body but do you know that you cannot possibly be your body? Your body fits well and you are not often aware of your body during the course of your day's activities. In fact, you have become increasingly unconscious of your body in your lifetime. For the most part, your body is just what you find yourself journeying through when you wake up each morning.

As a result of this, your body is likely to be taken for granted to a certain extent because it is always here and you always have it on. Again, you don't have the opportunity to take off your body to remind you that you are not the body and that you just *have* a body. The only reason you have forgotten that you cannot possibly be your body and you simply have a body is because you haven't had a daily reminder. This daily reminder would bring your awareness to the fact that you are not your body, reminding you over and over again that you just have a body.

Tuning in to the 'oneness' of life makes you fully aware of the fact that your body is not you. You see that it is just another tool for you to use, just like the thinking mind.

Your body enables you to feel, including feeling the world that is gently spinning in your chest, and helps you to learn the one lesson of life. When you have a thing, such as this pair of trousers or your body, and you take a moment to look into the truth of the matter, you will see that you cannot possibly *be* the thing that you *have*. You clearly see that the thing is not truly you; it is just something that you have, in this case it is something that you travel around in.

The Thinking Mind is in Overdrive

In its natural place, the mind is a well-balanced tool of the heart that is in harmony with life. This balanced mind will be called the **overall mind**, to set it apart from the unbalanced thinking mind.

The overall mind is selfless and is in touch with the 'oneness' of life. Therefore, it looks at life as a single community living for the good of the whole.

"Tuning in to the 'oneness' of life makes you fully aware of the fact that your body is not you. You see that it is just another tool for you to use, just like the thinking mind."

The thinking mind is a distorted part of the overall mind and because of this, it has thoughts of separation that are generally selfish and greedy. It is as if the thinking mind has been promised something about the world. It has felt sure of it, but then it was found out to be a lie. As a result, it understandably feels betrayed. The thinking mind now acts out that betrayal whenever it can. Like a small child throwing a tantrum to get attention, the thinking mind continues to 'act out,' because it has received attention by throwing tantrums before.

This distortion has been created by you because you have forgotten to put down the thinking part of the tool after you have used it and it has been given far too much attention. This is not something to worry about; it is simply something to stop doing!

This extra attention has sent the thinking mind totally out of balance and has caused it to be distorted and fractured, creating the unbalanced mental functioning of the brain. It is as if you are continually giving the left-hemisphere-based thinking mind huge doses of caffeine through the power of your attention and have forced it into overdrive. This distortion has created the conscious and unconscious aspects of the thinking mind and an ancient battle between the two.

In this battle, the thinking mind fights both to survive and to relax back to its natural state. This fight can be felt in the cycles of more intense inner conflict and mental activity as well as less intense mental activity. In the more intense cycles, you will experience the pressure to be free from the prison of the thinking mind much more keenly. The pain will push you towards looking for a way out; it will urge you to search for your true nature.

Neither side of this mental battle has anything to do with you, but you have accepted the idea that this battle is a battle within yourself. This battle has helped to reinforce the idea of separation. This idea is utterly incorrect!

This battle is another reflection of the misunderstanding of the one lesson of life; the lesson that your true nature is to live as one with this life. You have no choice or control over this battle because as we just mentioned, it has nothing whatsoever to do with you. It simply appears to be happening within you. As a result of this war being waged so close to you, it has been personified and has created the mind-made personality.

"This distortion of the mind has been created by you because you have forgotten to put down the thinking part of the tool after you have used it and it has been given far too much attention. This is not something to worry about; it is simply something to stop doing!

The reflection of this battle in your behaviour is the misguided belief that there is a need to stop the thinking mind to be at peace. This attempt to stop the mind causes you to feel that you are involved in this battle. The fact is that you are never called to stop the mind!

Trying to stop the mind is completely impossible and therefore, a waste of energy. It can also give you a physical headache and a build-up of frustration for your efforts. By tuning in to your true nature, the thinking mind will naturally slow down and there will be times when it stops all by itself, leaving nothing but peace.

However, until the thinking mind unifies with the overall mind, the thinking mind's distortion means that it cannot be trusted because it is so hyperactive and distracted. You cannot forcefully merge the thinking mind with the overall mind by willing this with your mind. That would create a catch-22 situation, with no way out. Tuning in to your true nature and taking your attention away from the thoughts is the only path to peace.

"Neither side of this mental battle has anything to do with you, but you have accepted the idea that this battle is a battle within yourself."

Stop Listening to the Thinking Mind

Each time you continue to listen to the harmful attitude of the thinking mind, even though you are aware of what you are doing, and you don't make the effort to tune in to the 'oneness' of life, it takes a little bit of extra strength to stay here in this moment again. This motion, of choosing not to make the effort, is similar to you putting more logs into the fire of your personal identification. It then takes a short burst of energy to burn the fuel out.

As mentioned before, when you tune in and surrender to the 'oneness' of your heart, the mind naturally settles down and comes into balance, with no fight or frustration involved. When you clearly see this battle of the thinking mind from outside of it, it creates the opportunity to permanently align with your heart. When you see this, it becomes obvious to you that only the powerful peace that you are, which is the backdrop to this battle, is true.

"When you clearly see this battle of the thinking mind from outside of it, it creates the opportunity to permanently align with your heart."

The power isn't in the mind; the power lies in you. This power is the power of your attention.

The fact that this thinking aspect of mind doesn't have any authority or influence over your true nature brings a profound feeling of relief and release. Your true nature is untouchable. This is part of its incredible beauty. You can truly relax and just let life be, in the complete faith that its magnificence cannot be touched or changed in any way.

Isn't it wonderful that you can relax in this way?

When you stop listening to the thinking mind and tune in to your true nature, your whole body will release every ounce of tension that has collected in your system. From this relaxed place, you will feel clarity in your whole perspective on life and witness changes for the better.

You can be sincerely thankful for the beauty and peace that you are, which you may just have touched on till now. This is real faith. You will only find setbacks happening if you shift your faith and trust back to believing the thinking mind and its idea of your personality, instead of faithfully trusting your heart.

"The power isn't in the mind; the power lies in you. This power is the power of your attention."

What You Have Learnt from Chapter Two

You *will* stabilise as this 'one.' It truly *is* your destiny.

Up until now, your life has been based on the original belief that you hold onto, of this idea of the package of your personality that you know as me, myself and I.

This one habit, of personally identifying with the thinking mind and its ideas leads to the creation of this person and to the selfish behaviour that keeps your identification as the person alive.

You are not called to judge your personality or attempt to change it. You just need to step outside of the identification with this person that you think you are and see the person as it is.

Acceptance, allowing and naturally letting go occur when you are tuned in and resting in the powerful peace that you are. This opens up the door to change.

You perform this personality. It is literally as if you are an actor reading lines and you have become embroiled in believing these lines as being what you truly think and feel.

As you live tuned in to your true nature, you will always focus your attention to what lies beneath the appearance of life and see the limitless depth and riches that are hidden there.

The thinking mind is not you; it is simply a tool that is at your disposal to use.

The power is in the pure potentiality that rests in the peace and stillness of the void within and is reflected to you by life. The only power that the mind has is when you give it the one power of your heart, through your attention.

You would be correct every time if, with each idea that came from the thinking mind, you said "That is untrue." Even if life appears to move in the same direction as that thought or idea, in the moment of thinking it, it was actually *not* true.

Tuning in to the 'oneness' of life makes you fully aware of the fact that your body is not you. You see that it is just another tool for you to use, just like the thinking mind.

This distortion of the mind has been created by you because you have forgotten to put down the thinking part of the tool after you have used it and it has been given far too much attention. This is not something to worry about; it is simply something to stop doing!

Neither side of this mental battle has anything to do with you, but you have accepted the idea that this battle is a battle within yourself.

When you clearly see this battle of the thinking mind from outside of it, it creates the opportunity to permanently align with your heart.

The power isn't in the mind; the power lies in you. This power is the power of your attention.

Chapter Three

How to Tune In to the Natural Happiness of Your True Nature

Here, in this chapter, you will be given an important key to living as your heart. This key is an invaluable one, which will assist you in your everyday life for the rest of your life, helping you deepen into the peace of your heart and to truly live in tune with life.

This chapter will show you that:

- The True Simplicity of Life is Already Yours

- Tuning In to the Sound of Silence

- Clarification of the Sound

- This is Not Nada Yoga

- The Still-Point of Your Attention

- The Flick of Your Attention, Back to the Sound

- The Weakening of the Motion Away

- See the Arising Experiences for What They Are

- Open Handed Living

- Who is in Control?

As always, take your time as you read to really take in and feel the peace of your heart, for yourself. This is an opportunity available to you in every moment and it will transform your life. Remember to relax and read with full attention and the entire matrix of your being.

The True Simplicity of Life is Already Yours

This is a book for action and change! As you continue to read this book, you will experience the truth of the words as they are soaked into your system.

Now that you have understood the basics of how life works, you are ready to learn the simplicity of uncovering your natural happiness. So far, you have learnt that you have absolutely nothing to overcome in life aside from the unconscious tendency to listen to, believe and identify with the thinking mind. This movement may sound like a mouthful, but it has all been done in one motion. This single motion is called personal identification.

Believing this personal identification has been a matter of habit and you can break this habit by consciously forming a new habit. This new habit involves tuning in to the truly powerful peace and beauty of the 'oneness' that you are. What's more, you will take to it like a duck to water because it's completely natural to you.

Tuning in to your true nature opens the space for you to become aware of the 'oneness' of life and to live as this 'one.' From this place of freedom, you will take responsibility for your creation and love your creation just as it is.

Your life is then free to return to balance.

The motion of tuning in gathers your energy into one focal point of truth, where your full power can come together and be lived at all times. By tuning in, you will divert the power of your attention away from both the inner world of the person and the outer world of the reflections of life.

This one simple motion of tuning in to your true nature will eternally change your life. You will be working against the influence of your personality and you will rise above the lifeless activity of personal identification. This can only happen without the involvement and disruption of the thinking mind. From this point on, your life will be rapidly enriched and you will be genuinely surprised at the benefits that come to you. Each day, greater rewards will show themselves in surprising ways.

By going to the core of life and living as this 'one,' you are eliminating the root of the problem, rather than trying to sort out the symptoms. You might imagine that going to the core of the issue would be harder than dealing with it one bit at a time, but this is not true. In fact, it is quite the opposite. Symptoms are endless and spring up eternally, while the root of the core remains.

Putting the power of your attention into the thinking mind has made everything seem complicated, when it truly is easy! The solution to each of your problems is so simple and it has been here all along.

So, are you ready to learn how to tune in to the truly unlimited potential and natural happiness of your true nature?

"The motion of tuning in gathers your energy into one focal point of truth, where your full power can come together and be lived at all times."

"This one simple motion of tuning in to your true nature will eternally change your life."

Tuning In to the Sound of Silence

You are now going to discover an extremely simple and easy approach to anchor into the beauty and joy of the 'oneness' of your true nature. All you need to do is tune in to the sound of silence.

You have heard this sound many times, which means that this sound is already well known to you. When you go somewhere that is totally silent, the silence can be almost loud. That loudness isn't coming from outside of you, it is coming from inside. Anything else that is heard is heard over the top of this sound.

Perhaps you have heard this sound as a child when swimming under water or maybe you have heard it at any time when both the internal and external reflections of life were momentarily silenced (such as after a heavy snow fall, a loud rock concert or in the silence of the mountains).

This sound of silence that is being referred to is the high-pitched sound that is always ringing in your ears and has been heard throughout your life.

REMEMBER

Remember a time when you have heard this sound.

This sound, which you have always known but never paid much attention to, brings you directly to the gateway through to the powerful peace that you are. It brings you deeply into your body and brings you in touch with the one meaning of life, into the true sense of purpose that you have been looking and searching for.

Whether this search for meaning has been made through a career, family, friends, travel or material possessions, the true search has been for the 'one' place in life, which you are to fill and no one else can.

The true search is always to find a way to live in natural happiness as one with your heart. You instinctively know that your heart has a perfect plan for you, which no one else can fulfil. It is your destiny. To live as one with your heart is the very thing that you have always wanted; it is the deepest core of your being.

The sound is the gateway through to this place.

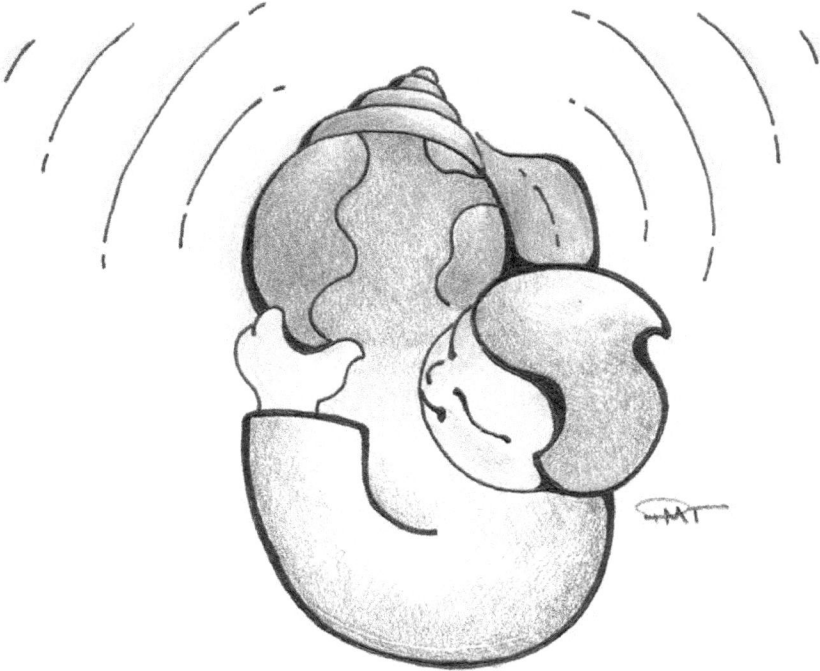

"An extremely simple and easy way to anchor into the beauty and joy of the 'oneness' of your true nature is to tune in to the sound of silence."

When you hear the sound, you are brought directly back into your body and into this eternal 'now' moment. Then, as you stay here, you naturally relax and surrender into the love of your heart and drop deeply into the powerful peace that you are.

When you rest in your true essence, you can clearly see your creation as it is. From this place, you can experience how all of creation has come out of the world in your chest and you can take complete responsibility for this. By doing this, you will naturally come to love all of life just as it is.

This sound acts as an anchor, which draws you away from your personality, brings you deeply back into your body and re-orients you to your natural happiness. Your full attention is then kept firmly grounded in this eternal 'now' moment, where the wonder and true love of life is.

"When you hear the sound, you are brought directly back into your body and into this eternal 'now' moment. Then, as you stay here, you naturally relax and surrender into the love of your heart and drop deeply into the powerful peace that you are."

No mental creations can survive in this vacuum of your true nature. As you tune in, the pictures in your mind dissolve and your focus of attention is brought back to what is really here; the eyelids, the sound, the room or space you are in. Tune in and wipe the pictures in your mind, create an empty space and re-wire the circuitry of your brain.

The sound runs through all of life. It is always here and is used by your heart to draw you past the hoax of your personality and the thinking mind. Tuning in to the sound brings you to rest in the natural peace and happiness that you are, which is silently beneath the creations of life.

The sound is unchanging, unmoving, all-encompassing, ageless, timeless and depthless. In fact, the sound is indescribable. It is a reflection of the timeless hum of your true nature; the timeless hum of existence. The sound is simply used by your heart to call you home.

Again, when you rest with the sound, your attention sinks deeper than your personality and you are set free to return to your truly natural place of rest.

In this place you are one with life.

The sound reaches through to the core of your being. It gently turns the way you see and experience life inside-out or at least, back to front. This sound shows you that life is a reflection of the beauty within you and that you have been living opposite to the natural flow of life, nearly in reverse. You have been mistakenly fighting an internal tug-of-war and struggling your way through life, instead of letting go of the fight and taking responsibility for your creation.

Taking responsibility, by tuning in to your true nature, brings natural peace, happiness and love to all of creation. The 'oneness' of life is destined to win, so why fight it when you can join it?

From this place of resting at the still-point and the sound, the thinking mind is no longer given the power of your attention, which liberates it from your grasp and the overall mind becomes integrated once more. This frees the mind to go back to its submissive position.

When you are no longer caught in the thinking mind, the perspective of being tuned in to the sound shows you that your personality is separate, temporary and merely layered on top of your true nature. Your personality is clearly seen as a reflection that is only here to teach you the one truth of life.

"This sound acts as an anchor, which draws you away from your personality, brings you deeply back into your body and re-orients you to your natural happiness. Your full attention is then kept firmly grounded in this eternal 'now' moment, where the wonder and true love of life is."

Clarification of the Sound

This is just to clarify: The sound is a high-pitched gentle ringing or buzzing 'tone' that is always naturally in your hearing. A similar sound is often referred to as 'Tinnitus' when heard loudly, although Tinnitus usually results from damage to hearing. However, this sound we are referring to is of your heart and can be heard by EVERYONE.

TUNE IN

Can you hear it right now?

Tune in and listen to the sound that is ringing (and singing) in your ears.

If you think about the sound too much and over-analyse it, that may make it more difficult to hear it. However, it is still here regardless of that. Simply relax and listen to the sounds that are around you. Then, listen closer than those sounds to a sound that is actually in your ear. It doesn't need to be loud or overly obvious. The words 'ringing' and 'buzzing' may have made you think that was the case. However, it is a subtle and gentle tone that is just here.

There are no vibrations as such; just a simple sound. It may take a moment to re-attune to it, but only a moment. If you have a bath and put your ears under the water or are in a totally silent room, or in the stillness of nature, the sound may be heard much more loudly. Therefore, ear plugs or ear muffs are recommended to begin with, to assist you in hearing the sound more loudly and distinctly and to re-familiarise yourself with the sound and the 'one' place of your true nature.

To integrate tuning in to the sound fully into your life, you can wear ear plugs in the morning as you wake up and prepare breakfast. With eyes open, tune in to the still-point of the sound and keep returning your attention to gently see your nose out of the corner of your eye. There is no need to go cross-eyed with this. Simply use your nose to remind your attention to rest deeper into your body. As your point of attention aligns to its rightful place once more, you can use the eyes as detailed later in this chapter.

This begins the day with you being tuned in to hear the sound loudly and clearly. It also reminds you to tune in to the sound during the rest of the day much more often.

Then, at times throughout the day, take a moment to put the ear plugs in to tune in to the sound and to relax while your heart guides you back to your true essence again. Wearing an ear plug in one ear while the other ear is unblocked, can also help you to tune in. This allows you to hear external sounds normally during your day. Only use the ear plugs whenever it is safe and comfortable to do so.

> "The perspective of being tuned in to the sound shows you that your personality is separate, temporary and merely layered on top of your true nature. Your personality is clearly seen as a reflection that is only here to teach you the one truth of life."

This Is Not Nada Yoga

In the yoga tradition, there is a practice called Nada Yoga. It is practised by closing your ears and listening to internal sounds. The instruction is to go with your awareness from the louder sounds to the more subtle sounds. In this practice, the sound is the object, so to speak, and it ends there.

It is important to point out that this is not the case here. The sound we are referring to is not interesting by itself. Its only function is to anchor you to the one true beauty that is beneath the sound and free of personal identification.

Listening to the thinking mind brings complication to your life. Don't make tuning in to the sound complicated. Do your best to keep it simple. Simply put in your ear plugs and take a walk to enjoy nature or have a lie-down or a warm bath to relax and settle into the beauty and joy of your true nature.

> "The sound is a high-pitched ringing or buzzing 'tone' that is always naturally in your hearing."

The Still-Point of Your Attention

As always, the mind tends to have wrong ideas. Generally, they are exactly opposite to what is true. In this case, it often makes an idea of the freedom of your true nature as being a vast, expansive, other-worldly and out-of-body experience. However, the initial tastes of true freedom are firmly grounded in the body in a tiny pinpoint of focus with no movement in any direction. This pinpoint will get smaller and more exact the longer you stay with it, until the confinement of the unbalanced personality drops away.

On the following pages is an exercise to give you an initial picture of where your attention naturally rests when you tune in to the still-point and the sound.

"Ear plugs or ear muffs are recommended to begin with, to assist you in hearing the sound more loudly and distinctly and to re-familiarise yourself with the sound and the 'one' place of your true nature."

Since this is such an important part of familiarising yourself with the sound and deepening into it, there is also a separate Still-Point audio included in the audio program, for you to practice with. (Available from: http://www.TrueNatureCentre.com/shortcut-to-inner-peace)

FEEL

Close your eyes and allow your body to release any tension and relax. Feel it become lighter and lighter with each out breath.

With your eyes closed, gently rest your eyes, focusing on the inside of your eyelids.

Now tune in to the sound that is singing in your ears.

You can easily hear this sound because it is always here, even when you are not consciously listening to it.

Take some time to let this sound become clear for you.

Keep your eyes looking straight ahead as you focus on the inside of your eyelids.

As you hear the sound, your attention is brought firmly into your body.

Now feel the origin of your attention as you see and hear.

Feel where your attention naturally comes from, as you hear the sound and look straight ahead.

FEEL

You are not to focus on where you think the sound is coming from, but instead focus on the origin of your attention.

To assist you with feeling this source of your attention, feel an imaginary laser beam of white light as it enters your forehead between your eyebrows at a slight downward angle and exits out of the back of your head at the base of your skull.

Now, another line of white light enters into the top of your head and goes straight down and through to your chest. This light is a fine line that is travelling straight down through your head to your neck.

The point where these two lines cross is deeply set in your head.

There is one more shaft of light, which enters in one ear and out of the other ear.

Where these three lines cross in your skull is the origin of your attention; the origin of your awareness.

Or you can imagine putting a finger in each of your ears until they touch. The point where the two fingers touch inside your head is the still-point of your attention.

This place is where your attention naturally comes from, so when you tune in with your eyes closed and rest with the sound, your awareness is naturally held here.

Feel this place and just rest. Let your hold on everything release and relax.

You are deeply grounded in your body.

Simply the back of the eyelids and the sound...

Relax and sink deeper into this still-point that the sound leads you to. Breathing and relaxing.

Now, stay here.............................

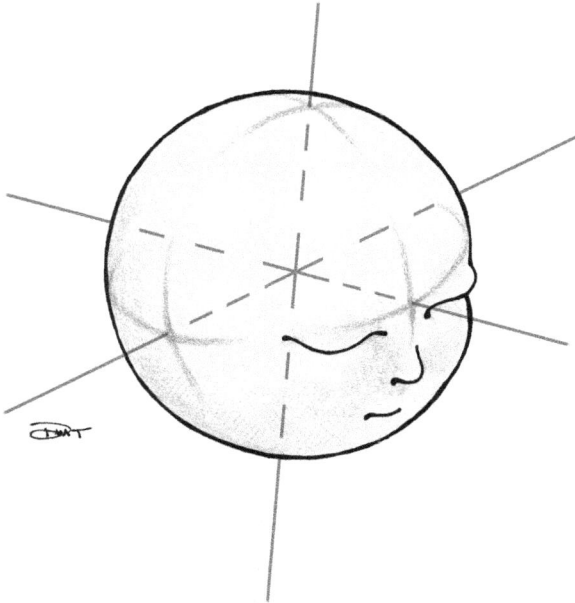

FEEL

As you stay tuned in with your eyes closed, feel a gentle connection pulling you into your heart.

This connection can be felt between this central place in your head and the centre of your chest. It will feel as if a warm energy is flowing through your body between the two.

(If you can't feel this energy at first, don't worry. It is always happening and you will come to feel it with time.)

It is very important to keep looking straight ahead, focusing on the inside of your eyelids. This helps to lock your attention in place and over time, the benefits of this will get stronger and stronger.

(If you are used to looking down rather than up or straight ahead, the muscles in your eyes may become slightly sore as you begin this. Persevere and this will swiftly pass.)

"The sound we are referring to is not interesting by itself. Its only function is to anchor you to the one true beauty that is beneath the sound and free of personal identification."

From this place, seeing will be happening; hearing will be happening; feeling will be happening; life will be happening; and your attention will be right here in this moment.

This still-point in your head is not a physical place. The physical is just used as a guide that is easy for you to relate to. Simply relax your attention on the sound and it will centre you into this place of awareness. Again, with eyes open, tune in to the still-point of the sound and keep returning your attention to gently see your nose out of the corner of your eye until you are familiar with this place.

The powerful peace that is underneath all of life is your truly natural state. Resting here in this still-point and then relaxing and melting into unity with your heart will show you that you know this place very well already. This place is this eternal 'now' moment.

Once this natural place of peace is felt, that is enough. As you rest your attention at this one still-point, you are at the gateway to your truly natural state of happiness.

Resting with the sound for a few moments, you sink deeper than your attention. Your body relaxes and you naturally surrender into the peace and 'oneness' that you are.

If you experience any resistance to the bodily relaxation and surrender, you can help it along by using your breath to relax the body. You can either sigh and relax on each out breath or give a couple of short, sharp exhalations and use these to relax any tensions that are being held on to. A comfortable chair or bed to relax into is also very helpful. If you are concerned about the possibility of falling asleep, don't be. Falling asleep may only happen initially, if at all, and your body will be relaxed and supported.

There is no need to sit up straight or to put your body through any pain to rest right here. So relax as much as possible and if you happen to fall asleep, then that is what is required for those moments. If sleep becomes a habit, then play music or open the door to the noises of your family or neighbours to prevent it.

"Listening to the thinking mind brings complication to your life. Don't make tuning in to the sound complicated. Do your best to keep it simple."

"It is very important to keep looking straight ahead, focusing on the inside of your eyelids. This helps to lock your attention in place and over time, the benefits of this will get stronger and stronger."

From this place of rest and relaxation, you will see that your attention, the thinking mind and the entire personality package are just naturally happening, without any input from you. As a result of this, you are no longer caught in the belief that you *are* these creations and you no longer personally identify with them.

The mind may wander as you begin to tune in to the sound. This is normal! Just see this wandering and also see that you don't actually go anywhere while this wandering occurs. You are still this 'one' and you are still right where you are at all times, regardless of the wandering of the thinking mind. The sound is here and you are here, whether your mind wanders or not.

Seeing this motion of the mind frees you from attaching any importance to the thoughts. The thoughts will then float past like a gentle stream on a summer's day. You can choose to dip your toe into the stream of the thinking mind or you can tune in to the sound, relax and bathe in the warmth of the one sun of your eternal heart. Either choice is fine and there is no pressure either way. However, now it is a conscious choice, with full moment-to-moment understanding of the consequences of each decision.

In truth, this is not a choice between your heart and life because your heart *is* life. This is the choice between living in conscious connection to the powerful heart of life or not. Not a tough choice really, is it?

"From this place of rest and relaxation, you will see that your attention, the thinking mind and the entire personality package are just naturally happening, without any input from you. As a result of this, you are no longer caught in the belief that you are these creations and you no longer personally identify with them."

The Flick of Your Attention, Back to the Sound

When tuning in is mentioned, it simply describes the flick of your attention back to the sound and relaxing into the still-point; nothing more. By simply staying tuned in, the magic of your true nature will loosen your grip on life and you can rest back into your true essence.

"You can choose to dip your toe into the stream of the thinking
mind or you can tune in to the sound, relax and bathe in the
warmth of the one sun of your eternal heart. Either choice is fine
and there is no pressure either way. However, now it is a
conscious choice, with full moment-to-moment understanding of
the consequences of each decision."

As mentioned, the sound is an anchor to the one beauty and joy of creation.
This anchor of the sound can be used by you to step outside of your
personality and sink deeper than your attention into the one powerful peace
that you truly are. From this place of spiritual freedom, you will see the
movement of your attention as it spins out of your body and into personal
identification with the creations of life.

When you see that you have been lost in thinking or in emotion, you will
find that in the very 'seeing' of this, there is space or consciousness and you
have the choice to tune in and rest with your heart once again. The motion
of tuning in to the sound shifts your attention away from your personality
and immediately stops the movement out and away from this one place of
rest. Again, you are not called to stop the mind.

Have you ever tried to stop the thinking mind? If you have, you will know
that trying to stop thoughts is completely impossible and therefore a waste
of energy. The more you try to stop them, the more attention you give to
the thoughts and they increase in their intensity.

Instead of all that effort, you are called to simply stay relaxed with the
sound, regardless of the motion of the thinking mind and all other creations
of life. You may almost see the mind out of the corner of your eye but your
attention will remain resting in the still-point of peace.

"In truth, this is not a choice between your heart and life because
your heart is life. This is the choice between living in conscious
connection to the powerful heart of life or not."

The Weakening of the Motion Away

The natural happiness of your true nature is not positive or negative. It is
the neutral, balanced still-point at the centre of life.

IMAGINE

Imagine a see-saw in a children's playground, with positive on one end and negative on the other end.

Your natural happiness is the balance point in the centre.

This still-point doesn't move or change and is only called happy, relative to normal daily living. More accurately, you can say that it is the absence of unhappiness, suffering and pain. In their absence, there is a simple and natural joy and then, freedom and peace.

Whatever suffering arises, you can be free of it by simply tuning in to the sound, which keeps your attention right here in this present moment. As you pin-pointedly focus into this sound, you are brought back into being the one true source of life. There is no particular feeling or experience of this 'oneness.' There is only the peace that is the backdrop of existence.

This single motion of tuning in is the key element, which bypasses countless years of searching and pain. When you tune in to the still-point and the sound and live your true nature on a consistent basis, you will find that you avoid a whole lot of internal tug-of-war suffering and the resistances of your personality. This tuning back in, over and over again whenever you need to do so, will weaken the motion away from being as one with your heart, until you stay here, relaxed in the true love of life and in the powerful peace that you are.

It will always be quicker and easier to use this internal sound, to tune in and come to rest in this moment, rather than any external sounds. This is because tuning in to the sound centres and grounds you in the body. The grounded body's function in this process is to hold you in place, so that you can move in life from this one point of freedom and live this 'oneness' in motion.

Once you are familiar with staying tuned in to the peace that you are, even if this inner sound of silence is obscured by other louder external noises, you will still be able to attune back to this still-point. At that stage, any sound, feeling or arising will be used as a reminder to tune in again and re-align your attention back into the body and rest as this 'one.'

Tuning in to the sound is not hard, serious or complicated in any way.

In fact, it's easy!

It's as easy as relaxing enough to let go of your hold on life and fall asleep. But instead of sleeping, you actually find yourself resting in the still-point of peace.

"This tuning back in, over and over again whenever you need to do so, will weaken the motion away from being as one with your heart, until you stay here, relaxed in the true love of life and in the powerful peace that you are."

In the first few moments of being tuned in to the sound, you need to hold your attention in the still-point by anchoring to the sound and keeping your eyes focused on the inside of your eyelids. This unplugs you from spinning out and into the thinking mind.

After a few moments of holding, the gravitational pull of thinking will cease. As soon as you stop here with the sound and out of the thoughts, you do not have to focus on holding still and can instead relax. Then, you will simply stay here in this moment and at rest.

You are simply called to hear the sound and stay with it and you will begin to live your true nature, which is already here and free. The motion of tuning in to the sound is like pointing behind someone and saying "Look at that!" and as they become distracted, you take a bite of their ice cream. This is what you are doing with your personality. You are anchoring your attention to something that the thinking mind cannot grab hold of, run with or even touch. This throws the mind off balance, allowing 'oneness' with your heart to quietly come back into your everyday life.

You must consciously volunteer for this privilege. To consciously volunteer, stay tuned in to the still-point and the sound so that your heart receives the clear, positive message of intention from you. By simply taking the power of your attention away from your personality, instead of building up your personality, you will be tearing it down and choosing to tune in and live the one truth of your true nature.

When your attention relaxes back to the sound and comes to being naturally held at rest here, you are brought directly back into being deeply grounded in your body and in this present moment.

Once your attention is back in your body, the space is created for you to clearly see the motion of the thinking mind. You are not called to look at the mind and watch what it is doing. You will simply see when your attention is with the motion of the mind and when it is clearly resting with the sound.

You will then become aware of times when you automatically pick up the personality again. You will be aware of when your attention is pulled out and away from the body into personal identification with this thinking aspect of mind and the creations of life.

"In the first few moments of being tuned in to the sound, you need to hold your attention in the still-point by anchoring to the sound and keeping your eyes focused on the inside of your eyelids."

Keep drawing your energy back to the focal still-point of this moment by tuning in to the sound. This stops the dispersal of your energy into the thinking mind and the appearances of life and prevents you from covering the present with ideas of the past and the future. Gently tuning in to the sound is only needed again when you see that your attention has returned to identifying with the mind and its thoughts once more.

Once the motion of your attention moving out from this place of peace has dissipated, only the simple resting here as this 'one' is left. Then no-one is here to hold attention on the sound. The sound will still be here, but you have no need for it as an anchor anymore because you are naturally happy and at rest as the 'one' that you truly are, with no motion of your attention pulling you away.

In those moments when the mind has come to rest, your body has come to rest and your personality is gone, you are left with an experience of a self-less state. This doesn't leave you living as an empty robot. Rather, this allows the free flow of your true nature through your body and your life becomes a true and natural expression of 'oneness.'

"You are simply called to hear the sound and stay with it and you will begin to live your true nature, which is already here and free."

See the Arising Experiences for What They Are

As you begin to rest in this still-point of the sound, keep your everyday life simple and do your best to stay out of the thinking mind as far as possible. The only way to stay out of the thinking is to tune in to the sound and focus solely on the still-point and nothing else.

Let everything else drop away as you determine to stay here.

"Keep drawing your energy back to the focal still-point of this moment by tuning in to the sound. This stops the dispersal of your energy into the thinking mind and the appearances of life and prevents you from covering the present with ideas of the past and the future."

"Once the motion of your attention moving out from this place of peace has dissipated, only the simple resting here as this 'one' is left."

As you rest here, you will begin to see the arising experiences (all external life and your inner world of the thinking mind, feelings, emotions, thoughts, your attention, personal identification) as a natural part of physical existence, similar to the blood that is pumped around in your body.

When you set out on a jog, the blood starts pumping faster and you feel it as it rushes through your veins. Similarly, the arisings of the mind that are reflected to you in your life are akin to the blood that flows through and creates the circumstances and experiences of this life. Stopping or changing them is impossible. They are a natural part of living.

These arising experiences have always been pumping around the system. You just haven't seen them in this manner before. In other words, you haven't seen them from the perspective of being outside of them, untouched by them and resting in the still-point of peace.

Staying tuned in to the sound takes the arising experiences for a jog, where they start flowing faster and become extremely clear. This opens the opportunity for you to see how life works. It opens the door for you to see the reality that the circumstances and experiences are created as a reflection of the spinning world in your chest and they are simply flowing through.

As you stay tuned in, you will also see that each arising feeling takes about 90 seconds to pass through your system and that it is only the additional judgements of the thinking mind that holds the feeling in place by labelling and distorting your perception of it.

The revelation that the arising emotional feelings pass through so quickly will help to free you from any fear of these feelings. And as your confidence and strength builds, the fact that nothing can touch this place of your true nature will be unmistakable.

"In those moments when the mind has come to rest, your body has come to rest and your personality is gone, you are left with an experience of a self-less state."

Open-handed Living

Focus on the still-point and the sound and life will take care of everything else. Stay tuned in through all arising experiences of life (all external life and your inner world), regardless of their appearance, and live gently, open-handed, with your full attention in this place. In this beautiful life, there is nothing to fear – ever. If you begin to feel fear arise, know that you have unconsciously given in to the belief of separation, which is from the thinking mind, instead of living as 'one' with your heart.

Fear is faith in the mind and what it tells you, instead of faith in your heart. This is the only misunderstanding of humanity and will be overcome by the simple act of tuning in to the sound. There truly is nothing to fear. Always remember that only the lies and deceit of the thinking mind can be lost when you tune in.

Welcome any realisations and insights that occur when you are resting at the still-point with the sound. Consistently staying right here reveals that any fear is untrue and any belief in the fear will be dropped. This may happen immediately or through natural hindsight a little while after the experience, but it will happen.

When you stay tuned in and rest here with your heart, you will see how the 'oneness' of life works. You will understand how the arising appearance of the personality is held in place by you pouring the fuel of attention into it and then, acting it out.

When you stay tuned in to the sound and you suck your attention back into this still-point, you will see and feel a gap between the peace that you are and the motion of the thinking mind and your personality. As this gap grows, you will notice that it is your choice to believe and follow this motion away from your heart or to simply stay here as this 'one' that you are. After this, you will stop attempting to act out this motion away, as you will view it as your creation or choice and not just as something happening to you. Anything that is seen, felt, known, experienced or understood must be left alone. Your true nature doesn't need to know or understand; it just is.

The more you look for proof of change, the more you block the magic of change that your heart brings. Simply stay tuned in to the still-point and you will find that the sound is the link between life as you have known it and the powerful peace that you truly are. Everything else is natural.

This tuning in will also help you to bring greater focus to whatever you happen to be doing throughout your day, as you will be firmly grounded in this moment.

"As you stay tuned in, you will also see that each arising feeling takes about 90 seconds to pass through your system and that it is only the additional judgements of the thinking mind that holds the feeling in place by labelling and distorting your perception of it."

"Fear is faith in the mind and what it tells you, instead of faith in your heart. This is the only misunderstanding of humanity and will be overcome by the simple act of tuning in to the sound."

Who is in Control?

You can truly relax and surrender to your heart. It is not a separate entity; it is the source of your creation. Therefore, no one can snatch the control out of your grasp. In reality, you never did have control of your life in the way you think of control. You just have the thinking mind's *idea* of control! Just like all of the other ideas from the thinking mind, the idea of control is all lies and hot air, entirely fake and truly impossible.

This is wonderful news because if you ever feel that you are in control, you can use that feeling as a reminder that you are not in touch with your one true essence. Similarly, when you feel that you like or dislike something, do your best to remember that it is usually only the thinking mind's way to undermine your quest for truth. The thoughts that are thrown up from the mind are often filled with these likes and dislikes, but they are not truly yours. So, you can relax and disregard them as soon as they appear.

What would happen if you completely dropped the ideas of control and personal preference? Is it possible that you would simply live free of any need to hold onto or demand a particular outcome or result from life?

IMAGINE & FEEL

Imagine not *having* to do anything but simply moving with the gentle flow of life just as it is.

Tune in and feel the relaxation and release of tension that level of freedom would bring to your everyday living, as you trust your heart to bring its power and joy into your life.

Your true nature is *that* free. It is already living itself through your body and through every other body on the planet. This is already happening. You have simply been convinced by the thinking mind that your personality is who you are. However, you always have the choice to suck your attention back to the still-point and the sound and tune in to where you will live as one with the heart of this life.

"Anything that is seen, felt, known, experienced or understood must be left alone. Your true nature doesn't need to know or understand; it just is."

Again, life is nothing other than the brilliance of your true nature simply living itself. You can see this reflected through the beauty and perfection of nature, as you tune in and gaze lovingly out of your window.

When you find yourself struggling with life, listen to the Powerful Peace Meditation audio to relax and melt into unity with your heart.

The Powerful Peace audio is a potent meditation that can be used to enhance and deepen your daily practice. Although not essential, it is highly recommended that you use this audio every day to familiarise yourself with your true nature and to set up a routine of tuning in to this 'one' in life. It is forty-eight minutes long, but is broken into smaller sections so that you can choose to listen to shorter parts of it.

"In reality, you never did have control of your life in the way you think of control. You just have the thinking mind's idea of control!"

What You Have Learnt from Chapter Three

The motion of tuning in gathers your energy into one focal point of truth, where your full power can come together and be lived at all times.

This one simple motion of tuning in to your true nature will eternally change your life.

An extremely simple and easy way to anchor into the beauty and joy of the 'oneness' of your true nature is to tune in to the sound of silence.

When you hear the sound, you are brought directly back into your body and into this eternal 'now' moment. Then, as you stay here, you naturally relax and surrender into the love of your heart and drop deeply into the powerful peace that you are.

This sound acts as an anchor, which draws you away from your personality, brings you deeply back into your body and re-orients you to your natural happiness. Your full attention is then kept firmly grounded in this eternal 'now' moment, where the wonder and true love of life is.

The perspective of being tuned in to the sound shows you that your personality is separate, temporary and merely layered on top of your true nature. Your personality is clearly seen as a reflection that is only here to teach you the one truth of life.

The sound is a high-pitched ringing or buzzing 'tone' that is always naturally in your hearing.

Ear plugs or ear muffs are recommended to begin with, to assist you in hearing the sound more loudly and distinctly and to re-familiarise yourself with the sound and the 'one' place of your true nature.

The sound we are referring to is not interesting by itself. Its only function is to anchor you to the one true beauty that is beneath the sound and free of personal identification.

Listening to the thinking mind brings complication to your life. Don't make tuning in to the sound complicated. Do your best to keep it simple.

It is very important to keep looking straight ahead, focusing on the inside of your eyelids. This helps to lock your attention in place and over time, the benefits of this will get stronger and stronger.

From this place of rest and relaxation, you will see that your attention, the thinking mind and the entire personality package are just naturally happening, without any input from you. As a result of this, you are no longer caught in the belief that you *are* these creations and you no longer personally identify with them.

You can choose to dip your toe into the stream of the thinking mind or you can tune in to the sound, relax and bathe in the warmth of the one sun of your eternal heart. Either choice is fine and there is no pressure either way. However, now it is a conscious choice, with full moment-to-moment understanding of the consequences of each decision.

In truth, this is not a choice between your heart and life because your heart *is* life. This is the choice between living in conscious connection to the powerful heart of life or not.

This tuning back in, over and over again whenever you need to do so, will weaken the motion away from being as one with your heart, until you stay here, relaxed in the true love of life and in the powerful peace that you are.

In the first few moments of being tuned in to the sound, you need to hold your attention in the still-point by anchoring to the sound and keeping your eyes focused on the inside of your eyelids.

You are simply called to hear the sound and stay with it and you will begin to live your true nature, which is already here and free.

Keep drawing your energy back to the focal still-point of this moment by tuning in to the sound. This stops the dispersal of your energy into the thinking mind and the appearances of life and prevents you from covering the present with ideas of the past and the future.

Once the motion of your attention moving out from this place of peace has dissipated, only the simple resting here as this 'one' is left.

In those moments when the mind has come to rest, your body has come to rest and your personality is gone, you are left with an experience of a self-less state.

As you stay tuned in, you will also see that each arising feeling takes about 90 seconds to pass through your system and that it is only the additional judgements of the thinking mind that holds the feeling in place by labelling and distorting your perception of it.

Fear is faith in the mind and what it tells you, instead of faith in your heart. This is the only misunderstanding of humanity and will be overcome by the simple act of tuning in to the sound.

Anything that is seen, felt, known, experienced or understood must be left alone. Your true nature doesn't need to know or understand; it just is.

In reality, you never did have control of your life in the way you think of control. You just have the thinking mind's *idea* of control!

Chapter Four

Building a Strong, Healthy Relationship with Your Heart

Welcome to Chapter Four. The emphasis of this chapter; **Building a Strong, Healthy Relationship with Your Heart,** is to show you how to do just that; how to strengthen your bond with your very own heart.

In this chapter you will learn to create:

- A Beautiful Relationship

- Natural Devotion

- Honesty and Trust will Bring You into Unity

- Speaking to Your Heart through Feeling

- Stop and See, Drop and Be

- Trust Your Heart to Direct You

- There is Only One Relationship

- A Solid Foundation

- Relaxation Sessions

- Putting Your True Nature First

Begin as you mean to continue; tune in and read with your entire being.

A Beautiful Relationship

Life is not as serious as the thinking mind makes it appear to be. Life is about joy. It is about uninhibited play and laughter. You also know now that life is beyond the thinking mind's idea of control, so you can rest and relax!

While you are resting in this relaxed state of peace, you are ready to progress to the next level and you can begin to nurture your creation. To do this, you must create a beautiful and healthy relationship with your heart. This relationship is happening already. However, because you have given the power of your attention to the thinking mind, you have been living as if you are at its command. Therefore, you have simply forgotten to breathe the power of your attention into developing this relationship. This is why there is such an unholy mess on this planet, but not to worry about that right now. By simply tuning in to the 'oneness' of your true nature, you will immediately be free of the mind's influence, free to live this powerful peace on a moment-to-moment basis.

Establishing this relationship with your heart helps you to take responsibility for your creation and love it from its core. This love can then flow out from the heart of life and embrace you back into itself, pulling you into your true nature.

This relationship also gives your *power of will* over to your heart and leaves your feeling of me, myself and I, in a more submissive position. This is essential until the thinking mind has the space to unravel and disconnect from your sense of personal identity.

At first glance, it seems like the thinking mind is in a dominant position and because of this misunderstanding, it has tremendous influence over your actions. This is why it is important for you to create a strong relationship with your heart and bring balance back into your life.

This gentle still-point of the sound allows you to move beyond fear, anxiety and the thinking mind. It gives you a clear understanding of what is true in life. It unifies the mind and calms your overactive bodily systems, creating a change that improves both your mental and physical health.

Remember that aligning to this still-point is the simple key to creating peace and freedom in your life and it can be done anywhere and at any time. Tuning in to the sound before reading this material – and whenever you are conscious of having reverted to paying attention to the thinking mind and its fight – will help you to gently absorb what you read.

With a true and close relationship with the 'oneness' of your heart, the thinking mind will return to its natural place as a tool that is obediently at your disposal. Transcending the thinking mind in this manner brings maturity and wisdom to your actions. It brings enough maturity and wisdom for you to live with a secure sense of humility. From this humbly respectful perspective, you will continue to take full responsibility for your creation and therefore, full responsibility for your life. Your relationship with your heart will then truly merge into 'oneness.'

Within the indivisible 'oneness,' there is no relationship. A relationship needs two to relate to each other. Without personal identification, there is only one – no other, no heart and therefore, no relationship. However, until this merging into 'oneness' happens, a strong relationship between the two is essential.

"Life is not as serious as the thinking mind makes it appear to be. Life is about joy. It is about uninhibited play and laughter."

Living this 'oneness' completes you and nothing from life is able to move or change this completion. Life becomes like water off a duck's back to you. Any trouble or difficulty is seen through and slides off you because you are completely protected. You are protected by the deep understanding that life is just a reflection of what is within you.

It is only when you come to live as one with your heart that this 'one' is reflected to you from life and you will permanently live in a powerful place of peace.

> "At first glance, it looks like the thinking mind is in a dominant position and because of this misunderstanding, it has tremendous influence over your actions. This is why it is important for you to create a strong relationship with your heart and bring balance back into your life."

Natural Devotion

Direct experience alone, holds the key to trust and faith in your true essence. Only you can truly experience this. It cannot be taught or bestowed upon you. You have to live it yourself.

Without building this wonderful relationship with your heart and connecting to it with your natural devotion, there may not be enough internal motivation for you to continue staying tuned in to the sound. This could only happen if you are still holding onto the thinking mind.

When you fully relax into tuning in to the sound and melting into 'oneness' with your heart in the powerful peace that you truly are, this devoted relationship is a natural love affair that is unstoppable.

Generally, if the thinking mind doesn't feel that enough is *in it for me,* it will lose interest in a very short period of time. The mind will then create distractions and excuses as to why you shouldn't bother tuning in.

If you believe the thinking mind's excuses and choose not to tune in to the sound, you might as well forget living your true nature and continue as you are. It truly is as clear-cut as that. You cannot have lasting change and still hang on to the old habit of personal identification. It is impossible.

> "Transcending the thinking mind brings maturity and wisdom to your actions. It brings enough maturity and wisdom for you to live with a secure sense of humility."

If this lack of motivation arises for you, and you are aware of the potential of this motion beforehand, you will not be fooled by it. Instead, you will see through it, ignore it and continue staying tuned in to the sound, regardless of how life appears.

There must be unfailing purpose behind your staying tuned in to the sound if you wish to bring it through to physical expression. Beneath this purpose must be a sure and firm faith that:

- Your true nature is already here.

- You have only to accept it.

- You are already completely free.

You will create this faith by your direct experience of tuning in and staying in the powerful peace that you are.

FEEL

Take a moment to feel into your body.

Tune in to the sound and relax.

Tap into this natural love and devotion and get all the experiential proof you need to gain the trust to help you persevere.

Feel this love as it flows through your entire system.

This natural love and devotion is not your personality's mental understanding and feeling of love. The emotions may be triggered as the mind feeds this mental understanding. However, this love isn't emotional love with highs and lows of experiential feelings. This love is the constant peace, which underlies feelings and experiences. It is the place that is untouched by any expression of life. As you give priority to tuning in to your true nature, you will come to live this ever-present peace in your everyday living.

"Direct experience alone, holds the key to trust and faith in your true essence. Tuning in to the sound as much as you possibly can is essential. It is only through this direct experience that a truly trusting relationship will be formed."

"When you fully relax into tuning in to the sound and melting into 'oneness' with your heart in the powerful peace that you truly are, this devoted relationship is a natural love affair that is unstoppable."

Honesty and Trust will Bring You into Unity

Again, a healthy relationship with your heart is built on trust and trust is created through experience. This is why tuning in to the sound as much as you possibly can is essential. It is only through this direct experience that a truly trusting relationship will be formed.

You cannot lie to your heart. It always knows what you are doing and why. So, you might as well be totally honest with yourself and accept whatever is happening. There is never anything to fear or anything real to lose.

Honesty goes hand-in-hand with trust because it is impossible to build a relationship of trust when you aren't being honest. Once you open up to honesty and accept your actions, you have the conscious choice to continue in the same manner or do something different this time.

If you feel that your heart has caught you in a lie, for example, if you pretend not to notice that you are not tuned in to the still-point of peace, shaky ground is created. This shaky ground opens the opportunity for the thinking mind to bring doubt, fear and confusion to the picture.

"Honesty goes hand-in-hand with trust because it is impossible to build a relationship of trust when you aren't being honest. Once you open up to honesty and accept your actions, you have the conscious choice to continue in the same manner or do something different this time."

Speaking to Your Heart through Feeling

Learn to notice the difference between the emotional responses to the thoughts (such as doubt, fear and confusion) and the free feeling of your heart; the raw, core feeling. These core feelings are not emotional feelings, but those deep-down feelings that are free from any thought.

Mind-made emotions are generally felt in the diaphragm area or solar plexus, which is just below your physical heart where your ribs end and your abdomen begins. When you let the thoughts settle by tuning in to the sound, these emotions will subside and lose their power.

Like all feelings, emotional feelings only last about 90 seconds. If they are dragging on any longer than that, it means that you are holding them in place. You do this whenever you are giving these feelings interpretations or by feeding them with your attention. However, if you are experiencing deep grief, you may feel waves of emotion and then each wave will last about 90 seconds. At these times, do your best to relax as much as you can and feel the waves as they come and go. If you let the waves pass through naturally, they will come to an end with greater ease.

Core feelings are commonly felt either in the centre of the chest or deep in the belly or 'hara' just below the belly button. Frequently, these feelings are referred to as intuition or a gut feeling.

Even though your heart is not the feeling, it talks to you using feelings. As in every relationship, it is vital to learn to listen and communicate with your heart. Even though you are always in full communication already, you haven't been listening to what your heart is telling you. It is always telling you the one lesson; that you are already this 'one' powerful peace that rests beneath the reflections of life and you can freely live as this 'one' right now.

Listen and don't be afraid. Your heart can see the big picture and has a perfect plan for your success. If you are unsure whether a feeling is from the thinking mind or from your heart, take a moment to tune in and let it show you. Ask your heart, using internal prayer, if you're not sure what its movement means. Speak honestly and openly so that miscommunication is avoided.

FEEL

Feel where the feeling is coming from in your body.

If it is coming from your solar plexus, feel into your chest or your '*hara*' and you will feel that these areas are calm.

If it is coming from your chest or '*hara*' and you feel relaxed, you can trust that it is your heart speaking to you.

Never keep anything bottled up because you are afraid your heart won't approve of it. Your heart doesn't judge. It is totally accepting of everything just as it is. It will however move you to do something differently if need be. Just make sure you are listening!

Tuning in is the perfect way to open up to life and listen to it. If you are closed to the negative feelings, then you are also closed to the positive feelings because truly, all feelings are the same. They simply have different labels given to them by the thinking mind. Therefore, if one core feeling is held back, then the rest will also be held back to the same degree.

When you find this holding back or suppression of feelings occurring, it can stoke the fire of the thoughts and the emotions that arise from them. If you get stuck in any one feeling and stay there, it can distort and numb your feeling capacity, draining you of energy and focus. Don't try to control these feelings; experience them! Unrestricted, these feelings quickly come and go.

TUNE IN & RELAX

Use your breath to help you to relax into any feelings that arise.

Tune in to the sound and continue breathing normally.

Now use the out-breath to simply relax and melt deeper and deeper into your body.

Each exhalation brings more relaxation and release from the stresses of life. From this relaxed place, feelings will freely move through your system.

"Learn to notice the difference between the emotional responses to the thoughts (such as doubt, fear and confusion) and the free feeling of your heart; the raw, core feeling."

Stop and See, Drop and Be

Going against the repetition of the thinking mind by tuning in to the 'oneness' of life is a powerful force for change. Both, events in life and the thinking mind along with its judgement of these events set up conditions in the body where weak spots are created in your energetic system. These weak spots develop into emotional patterns that you find recurring in your life.

As you tune in and live from the beauty of your true nature, you find yourself going deep within you to the core of the one habit of listening to the mind and healing that habit. This directly reflects in your physical life by going to the core of your being and healing the weak spots from the inside. However, when the thinking mind is acting out these emotional patterns and being loud, it can distract you from tuning in and move you away from living the natural happiness of your heart.

At these times, to clear any mental agitation, simply stop for a moment and see what is happening within the mind and the emotional system. As you see the arising experience, relax into it being just the way it is. This seeing and relaxation allows the mental or emotional feeling to just be here, without any fight or effort to change it in any way. This stimulates the energy within the mental or emotional pattern and stirs it up so that it can be felt. As you naturally take responsibility in this manner, your energy rebalances itself, freeing your attention to relax back into 'oneness' with your heart.

From this relaxed place, you will see that the feelings and emotions are not who you truly are. They are simply part of the one package of the person. As a natural result of this seeing, you will have stepped out of the feelings and will no longer be personally identifying with them.

ACTION

To do this now, stop and tune in to the still-point and the sound. Rest your eyes, focusing on the inside of your closed eyelids and hear the sound.

Now allow an emotion or a memory to come into your awareness. It could be something pleasant or painful from your past or anything that is arising right now.

As you see this feeling or emotion, concentrate on accepting the feeling, allowing any thoughts that may be arising and embracing the body's reaction to those thoughts.

Simply relax and open your awareness, and allow it to be here.

Now, step out of the feeling and see the feelings and emotions as part of the person, as one whole unit, rather than separating it out into elements of certain characteristics.

As you do this, you can see that these feelings and emotions are not who you are. They are simply part of this package that you have identified yourself as being.

In the moment of seeing that these feelings and emotions are not you, they naturally fall away. You are no longer holding on to them as being a part of you and in that moment, you have automatically decided to drop them and let them go.

Now, stay here and sit in the space of emptiness and peace that is your true nature. You can hear the sound and feel the relaxation and beauty that is resting below all experiences.

You can stop and see, drop and be at any time and in any place. It is a silent inner release that happens in a matter of moments and the more you relax into this process, the quicker it will become. If you feel resistance to allowing the feelings or emotions to just be here, you can use a simple mantra such as "Thank you for this beautiful mind" or "Thank you for this wonderful person" or "Thank you for this perfect 'one' that I am." Saying this mantra out loud with a happy smile is great if you are in the position to do so. If not, smile on the inside and silently repeat the mantra to yourself.

"Wearing a happy smile is great. If you are in the position to, smile."

You can also take responsibility for your creation of the thinking mind and forgive yourself by repeating "I'm sorry" and "I love you" as you relax and release.

Again, the personality is one single package and it is just the mind that creates different expressions of this package. Stopping and seeing, dropping and being assists the unconscious aspects of your system to acknowledge, accept and embrace the thinking mind and the personality. It helps to re-program the unconscious mind, release any feelings of being stuck or feelings of hardship and will help your system to open up and anchor into this moment again.

Before, during and after this process, tune in as best you can and simply allow yourself to fall into the silence of your true nature. Along with tuning in, stopping and seeing as well as dropping and being will help you let go of the tug-of-war rope and bypass any resistance to the way life is in this moment. It will help you surrender to the beauty of this moment, just as it is.

Please understand that this process may bring old emotional energies to the surface for you to feel and as you stay tuned in and as one with your heart, these trapped energies will be released. There is no need to see any details of where these trapped energies are coming from. The thinking mind will always lead you astray here by over-dramatising things. Any details seen, however, are shown for you to learn the one lesson of life and also to see the motion of the person and the thinking mind. You will find maturity, inner strength and spiritual freedom from these true insights. There is no need to over-indulge with this process. It is simply for relief from an overactive stream of thoughts and emotions.

"The personality is one single package and it is just the mind that creates different expressions of this package. Stopping and seeing, dropping and being assists the unconscious aspects of your system to acknowledge, accept and embrace the thinking mind and the personality."

Trust Your Heart to Direct You

Trust your heart enough to allow it into every aspect of your everyday living. Also, allow the space to be shown the best direction to take. You are given this one life. This is what you've got. Listen to it and don't be afraid!

Often, you can feel what your heart is urging you to do, but you choose to listen to the thinking mind. You do this either by directly listening to the thoughts or listening to someone else, who is reflecting the thinking mind to you externally.

Put your heart's opinion first every time, regardless of what the mind says about it. As you do this, trust grows within your relationship and your heart's move will become louder and more obvious to you.

If you don't reach out and ask, you don't receive. Remember, you will never be rejected or turned away. Tuning in to the sound and unifying with your heart is how you can easily open up to receiving. From this place of freedom, you relax back into the powerful peace that you are and every desire is fulfilled.

In time, as you are unified with your heart, its move will be your move because you are living as 'one.' When you have this purpose in your life, the whole universe naturally moves in the direction of fulfilling this purpose.

> "Put your heart's opinion first every time, regardless of what the mind says about it. As you do this, trust grows within your relationship and your heart's move will become louder and more obvious to you."

There is Only One Relationship

There is one relationship; it is your relationship with your heart, the true source of life. All relationships that you have had in your life with your mother, father, brother, sister, teacher, friend, co-worker or lover are a direct reflection of this one relationship.

Your internal relationship with your heart and the external reflection of relationships are both important. They both have many secrets to reveal to you about your choices and actions. What you see happening in one, you will see is directly reflected in the other, showing you the many ways that you play out the one habit of listening to the thinking mind.

Again, regardless of their appearance, every one of the external relationships you have is a reflection of your one relationship with your heart. Even the best of these relationships can only ever be a pale reflection of the joy of unifying with this 'one.'

Owing to this mirror effect, you can look to past or present external relationships to help you see what it is that you do when you relate to others. You can use these relationships as a guide to show you how you *deal* with relationships. This insight will help you understand what you are doing to avoid learning the one lesson of life.

"In time, as you are unified with your heart, its move will be your move because you are living as 'one.' When you have this purpose in your life, the whole universe naturally moves in the direction of fulfilling this purpose."

LOOK

Take a moment now to tune in and look at the limiting beliefs that you carry around about relationships and see where they originate from.

As you are shown these beliefs, see that they are there to teach you the one lesson; the lesson that you have forgotten to live as one with life.

Intimate love relationships are the closest reflection of your relationship with your heart because the patterns are often very obvious once you begin to look. The other relationships in your life can seem more complicated because there are so many differing agendas involved.

For this next exercise, it's best to keep it simple and focus on love relationships. These relationships can show you exactly what you do to sabotage relationships.

LOOK

Close your eyes and tune in to the sound.

Keep your eyes looking straight ahead, focusing on the inside of your eyelids.

Now, bring your most recent past or present relationship to mind.

Picture the other person's face and see what thoughts and feelings arise.

Look to this past or present relationship and see a pattern of behaviour that you act out each time.

LOOK

Do you try to control the relationship? Do you prefer to be controlled? Or is there balance within the relationship?

What do you look for in a partner? And why?

Do you give these attributes *to* your partner?

See the thoughts that you listen to about this person and about yourself.

See the character you become and the roles that you both take on within the relationship.

Then in this same way, take the time to look at any other previous relationships that you have been involved in.

Again, look at the behavioural patterns and the roles that were being played out. See why the relationship came to an end and how you both dealt with the situation.

This is a very powerful exercise and worth taking your time with. It shows you that you have always been responsible for listening to the thinking mind and considering what it says as the truth.

This is the signature of the one pattern that you act out in all areas of your life. You repeat this one pattern in many different disguises. As you tune in and relax into this relationship with your heart, you will clearly see this one habit that is being repeated.

Viewing this requires honesty. "For what?" you may ask. It needs honesty to:

- Truly see your actions and motivations,

- See where the thinking mind comes in and makes a mess and

- See what your particular signature of mess looks like.

It also shows you that you now have a choice! Once you have seen this signature in one relationship, you will find that this same signature runs through every relationship that you presently have or have ever had, to some degree or another. This includes your relationship with your heart.

The details may change slightly. However, the signature is unmistakable as soon as you see it. This same signature acts as a barrier that you hold in place, which your relationship with your heart can't get through. As you tune in and see these patterns of behaviour, you will easily step out of these behaviours and the patterns are then free to dissolve as you sink into the beauty of living from the powerful peace that you truly are.

RELAX & RELEASE

Relax and accept the past.

You will find that the mind's influence and these beliefs about the past will be set free.

"There is one relationship; it is your relationship with your heart, the true source of life."

A Solid Foundation

By reading and acting on what is suggested in this book, you are creating a solid foundation for this relationship with your heart. As you nurture this relationship, you will experience it grow and deepen. It will become irresistible and you will witness the benefits of it in every part of your life.

This relationship will draw you into itself if you let it because that within you, which knows and loves your heart, is the heart loving itself. To be aligned to your heart consciously is what you crave most in life because it brings you to this 'one' (your true nature). Every fibre of your being is calling you to live in alignment with this 'oneness' of creation. Again, living in unity with your heart is the only lesson there is and it is repeated in every area of your life.

This irresistible love for the truth in you is not dependent on anything. This love is not a result, an experience or a doing. It is simply your heart's true love for itself that rests beneath the appearance of life.

Tuning in to your true nature will kindle this love into many moments and will ignite a burning fire of irresistible devotion in your chest. This devotion will then consume all that is false in your life.

"By reading and acting on what is suggested in this book, you are creating a solid foundation for this relationship with your heart. As you nurture this relationship, you will experience it grow and deepen."

There is no particular place you need to go to for this relationship because it is already within you. Therefore, this relationship is with you wherever you go. But, as with any new relationship, it is important to initially find a quiet place where you can be together with your heart. Find a place where you can get in touch with each other more deeply.

After this courtship phase, trust is built in the relationship. You will begin to see the 'oneness' of life and invite your beloved heart out with you into your everyday actions. Then, the love of your heart will continuously shine into every cell of your being.

This love will grow to the point where you will live with your heart in every moment of your day. It will grow so much that you will want to share your life with your heart and live as one with it, simply because it is the natural thing to do. There is no life without it!

You must have already experienced a spontaneous moment when the love of your true nature took over your life, even if it was by simply viewing a beautiful sunset. The mind clears, your body relaxes and it feels that you just melt right into love. That is a moment of truth, a moment of freedom. It is irresistible.

"There is no particular place you need to go to for this relationship because it is already within you. Therefore, this relationship is with you wherever you go."

Relaxation Sessions

As was just mentioned, no particular conditions are required for you to live as one with your heart (your true nature). This 'oneness' already exists beneath any and every thing.

However, it is strongly recommended to add two, thirty-minute relaxation sessions (preferably lying down or, if that is not possible, sitting) to your daily routine. These relaxation sessions will give you the space to tune in to the sound and step out of the personality package. This will help you re-familiarise with the powerful peace that you are.

You will find yourself spending time resting as your true nature. As a result of this, your body will be rested and rejuvenated too. The body has a natural ability to heal itself; it only needs the space to do so.

As mentioned before, the Powerful Peace Meditation audio is divided into sections to help you to build up to these thirty-minute sessions.

It is best to read when you are awake and alert and listen to the audios and relax, when you are not.

There are times throughout the day, where your physical energy is at a high or a low. Often, just after a meal you may experience a 'low' period, where the body is busy digesting food. This digestion takes energy from the body and causes a slight deficiency in your energy levels. Mid-afternoon is also a natural, low-energy time.

Knowing this, you can organise the thirty-minute lie-down sessions so that they are in your natural energy slump times. Use these times to allow the body to relax and rest as you sink deeply into the beauty of your true nature. Again, a short nap isn't a problem if that is what your body needs. However, the purpose of these relaxation sessions is to consciously tune in and rest here.

In a work situation, if you have your own office and the opportunity to do so, you can lie on the floor. If not, you can use your car or ask to use some other area for this purpose.

For the first six weeks, during these thirty-minute sessions, it is preferable to have your eyes closed and use ear plugs or ear muffs to tune in to the sound. Your eyes can be open at times if you like, although it may be easier to relax into the sound with your eyes closed.

It may feel like the mind gets busier with eyes closed, but you are simply realising how busy the thinking mind truly is when you are not being distracted by the external world. Remember that the mind is not you and you can simply rest despite the mind being busy, letting it play out without giving it any attention. Feed as much attention as you can into relaxing into the sound instead.

During the lie-down sessions, allow the day to drain away and the sound will be all that is left. Nothing else truly exists. This peace that you are is always here beneath existence and brings a new perspective of natural happiness and balance, if tuned in to consistently. You are not objectifying this peace. You are simply returning only to the sound and the inside of the eyelids.

"After this courtship phase, trust is built in the relationship. You will begin to see the 'oneness' of life and invite your beloved heart out with you into your everyday actions. Then, the love of your heart will continuously shine into every cell of your being."

TUNE IN & RELAX

Be still and listen.

With closed eyes, just let your eyes rest their gaze straight ahead on the inside of the eyelids and relax easefully into the sound.

Don't create something out of the peace. It is only the sound that exists. Everything else is a burden that distracts you from the freedom of your true nature.

Habitual use of the Powerful Peace Meditation audio will be helpful in guiding you to build a strong relationship with your heart in this 'one' place of your true nature. Thereafter, however, simply tuning in to the sound is the only thing that you need to do to stop here, in this moment.

"It is best to read when you are awake and alert and listen to the audios and relax, when you are not."

Putting Your True Nature First

In a healthy relationship, everyone needs to make compromises. Your heart is and has been compromising for a very long time. It has loved you enough to let you act out every lie that you have ever wanted to. Now it is your turn to love your heart enough to put your true nature first and tune in to the 'oneness' of life. This is the way to give respect to your heart.

Go against what the thinking mind says, tune in and follow the influence of your heart instead. This doesn't mean you should feel like you're losing out on being yourself. Actually, it is the opposite that is true.

You don't have to pretend to like something you don't. Pretence has nothing to do with your true nature. You also do not need to stop meeting your friends or drop out of activities you truly love. Feel free to develop new talents or interests, make new friends and move forward. Just take your heart with you. Live as this 'one' that you are and keep your heart at the forefront of your life.

You don't need to talk about it to others if you don't feel moved to. This relationship is yours to develop in whatever way works for you. It is a purely intimate affair.

"For the first six weeks, during the thirty-minute lie-down sessions, it is preferable to have your eyes closed and use ear plugs or ear muffs to tune in to the sound. Your eyes can be open at times if you like, although it may be easier to relax into the sound with your eyes closed."

A healthy relationship with your heart is fun. It isn't there to make you feel good about yourself, although it will certainly do so. Building this relationship will demolish any struggle with self-esteem problems because a natural feeling of deep contentment and happiness is an added benefit. This feeling won't be egotistic or arrogant. It is a feeling of inner strength and is simply a reflection of the 'oneness' of your beautiful heart.

By the time you finish reading this material, you will be able to easily live as this 'one'!

FEEL

Doesn't it feel fantastic to have such a rewarding relationship, budding and growing between you and your heart?

This is a relationship of love, trust and support that you can always rely on.

Tune in to the sound and feel the warmth growing in the core of your being and joy and gratitude blossoming through your body in anticipation of living the deep peace, beauty and natural happiness that you truly are.

"During the lie-down sessions, allow the day to drain away and the sound will be all that is left. Nothing else truly exists."

What You Have Learnt from Chapter Four

Life is not as serious as the thinking mind makes it appear to be. Life is about joy. It is about uninhibited play and laughter.

At first glance, it looks like the thinking mind is in a dominant position and because of this misunderstanding, it has tremendous influence over your actions. This is why it is important for you to create a strong relationship with your heart and bring balance back into your life.

Transcending the thinking mind brings maturity and wisdom to your actions. It brings enough maturity and wisdom for you to live with a secure sense of humility.

Direct experience alone, holds the key to trust and faith in your true essence. Tuning in to the sound as much as you possibly can is essential. It is only through this direct experience that a truly trusting relationship will be formed.

When you fully relax into tuning in to the sound and melting into 'oneness' with your heart in the powerful peace that you truly are, this devoted relationship is a natural love affair that is unstoppable.

Honesty goes hand-in-hand with trust because it is impossible to build a relationship of trust when you aren't being honest. Once you open up to honesty and accept your actions, you have the conscious choice to continue in the same manner or do something different this time.

Learn to notice the difference between the emotional responses to the thoughts (such as doubt, fear and confusion) and the free feeling of your heart; the raw, core feeling.

Wearing a happy smile is great. If you are in the position to, smile.

The personality is one single package and it is just the mind that creates different expressions of this package. Stopping and seeing, dropping and being assists the unconscious aspects of your system to acknowledge, accept and embrace the thinking mind and the personality.

Put your heart's opinion first every time, regardless of what the mind says about it. As you do this, trust grows within your relationship and your heart's move will become louder and more obvious to you.

In time, as you are unified with your heart, its move will be your move because you are living as 'one.' When you have this purpose in your life, the whole universe naturally moves in the direction of fulfilling this purpose.

There is one relationship; it is your relationship with your heart, the true source of life.

By reading and acting on what is suggested in this book, you are creating a solid foundation for this relationship with your heart. As you nurture this relationship, you will experience it grow and deepen.

There is no particular place you need to go to for this relationship because it is already within you. Therefore, this relationship is with you wherever you go.

After this courtship phase, trust is built in the relationship. You will begin to see the 'oneness' of life and invite your beloved heart out with you into your everyday actions. Then, the love of your heart will continuously shine into every cell of your being.

It is best to read when you are awake and alert and listen to the audios and relax, when you are not.

For the first six weeks, during the thirty-minute lie-down sessions, it is preferable to have your eyes closed and use ear plugs or ear muffs to tune in to the sound. Your eyes can be open at times if you like, although it may be easier to relax into the sound with your eyes closed.

During the lie-down sessions, allow the day to drain away and the sound will be all that is left. Nothing else truly exists.

Chapter Five

A New Perspective on Life

In this chapter you will learn some new perspectives on life. You will learn about how your belief in the thinking mind is the ONE habit that blocks you from simply being your true nature. You will also learn about the power and limitlessness of your attention and how to use this to strengthen your relationship with your heart.

Here are the main things you will learn about here:

- Respecting Yourself

- Unhealthy Relationships

- Projecting the Thinking Mind onto Your True Nature

- Relationship Struggle

- Again, Stop Listening to and Believing the Thinking Mind

- The Workings of The Mind

- Filtering Out Junk Thoughts

- Your Attention is Limitless

- Creating an Attention Power-pack

- Strengthening the Power-pack of Your Attention

Remember to tune in to the peace and fullness of your heart before you begin to read. This will help you to fully absorb this material. Whenever you realise that your attention has wandered, relax and simply tune in again and rest in the powerful peace of your true nature.

Respecting Yourself

Respect in your relationship with your heart shows that you value this relationship. Respect is shown by your willingness to:

- look at the reflections of life

- learn the 'one' lesson

- understand the truth that your heart is teaching you

Your heart always respects your boundaries, allowing you to play things out as you listen to the influence of the thinking mind. That is why it is up to you to move past these boundaries. What's more, your hand will quietly be held all the way.

Simply step out of the mind and tune in to the 'oneness' of your true nature, and let the powerful peace that you are move into your life, whatever the weather may be. Your heart will support you in all conditions and not only in the tough times. It is there as a shoulder to cry on when you lose your job and to celebrate with you when you get a better one. Just as it supports you, you can give back by tuning in to your true nature and putting it ahead of all things.

You need to have this 'give-and-take' in your relationship. Both sides of this coin of 'give-and-take' are merely reflections of each other. They are both needed because, as always, without one reflection, it is as if you have covered over one of the mirrors in life's hall of mirrors and you remove the opportunity for the opposite reflection.

'Openness' to your heart allows 'give-and-take' to happen. Of course, you don't have to keep count and make sure things are exactly even. But you will know if there is balance and openness or not, because you will feel it. Your heart will tell you and tuning in will help you to listen.

> "This relationship is yours to develop in whatever way works for you. It is a purely intimate affair."

Unhealthy Relationships

As you relax deeply into building a healthy relationship with your heart, it is helpful to see what an unhealthy relationship looks and feels like. This unhealthy relationship may be between you and the thinking mind.

A relationship is unhealthy when it involves mean, controlling, abusive or disrespectful behaviour. The thinking mind uses mean language, verbal insults and nasty put-downs towards you on a continual basis.

FEEL

Experience how weak and hopeless these insults and put-downs make you feel.

It is very similar to an abusive relationship, where, through familiarity, you have become so obedient that the thinking mind is able to push you around, without any effort on your part to make any move to get clear of the situation.

These feelings of weakness and hopelessness are warning signs of the thinking mind's relentless abuse. The thinking mind has no power in and of itself, however. You are the one placing the power of your attention into it and this has caused this distortion.

This distortion is a sign that the relationship that you have with the thinking mind is unhealthy and it is time to leave it behind. You can now easily live free from this dictatorship and you can use this 'seeing' to learn how awful an unhealthy relationship feels.

The difference between a healthy and an unhealthy relationship lies in how well you deal with the challenges that you face in that relationship. You can work through all challenges and you can widen your perspective on whatever is going on by taking the time and space to tune in to your true nature.

Now, as you build a beautiful, strong relationship with your heart, you can feel the wonder of this healthy relationship much more deeply. This feeling of wonder will bring a profound feeling of gratitude in knowing that your glorious heart is now your best friend in life.

FEEL

Tune in and feel how wonderful and peaceful life is when you are living from the beauty of your heart.

Feel the gratitude within you for this strong relationship.

You can now live consciously, tuned in to your true nature. As a result, you will forgive yourself for these past mistakes because they were unconscious.

"Now, as you build a beautiful, strong relationship with your heart, you can feel the wonder of this healthy relationship much more deeply. This feeling of wonder will bring a profound feeling of gratitude in knowing that your glorious heart is now your best friend in life."

Projecting the Thinking Mind onto Your True Nature

Making your true nature a *'something'* allows the thinking mind to project familiarity. Have you ever heard the saying "Familiarity breeds contempt"? As your true nature is always here and can be completely relied upon, it can become easy to create familiarity.

Be aware of this and do your best not to project anything onto your true nature in any way. Your heart is also not an object. It is the sea of potential from which all creation arises.

Projecting any *'thing'* onto your heart creates doubt and uncertainty, leading to distrust. You can already see how you have personalised the mind and how this has caused a tremendous pain by identifying with the personality. Please, don't do it again with your heart!

At the beginning, relationships require time and energy to grow. Every relationship needs effort to keep it strong and positive. Even a wonderful, strong relationship with your heart can be destroyed through neglect.

If you personalise your relationship with your heart and project it onto a person or thing, you will begin to distort what your heart is showing you. This projection will cause confusion, anger and disappointment. These emotions will poison this beautiful relationship.

Often, the thinking mind misguidedly projects your relationship with your heart onto and invests it into a spiritual teacher. This person is put on a pedestal and is looked up to and revered through this projection. However, when this person is perceived to let down the thinking, it causes unnecessary heartache. This can be prevented by not letting any erosion of your intent or your integrity to stick with that intent.

Just as in any other relationship, you have made a promise to your heart to create and nurture your relationship. If you break this promise by having an affair with the thinking mind, it weakens the trust within the relationship. It sends the signal to your brain and through your system that you are not committed to living your true nature and this signal creates confusion in your system. The thinking mind then uses this disturbance as an opportunity to sabotage the deepening of your loving connection with your heart. To put it another way, the re-programming of the hemispheres of your brain cannot be rewired if you continue to rebuild the existing connections.

"Do your best not to project anything onto your true nature in any way. Your heart is also not an object. It is the sea of potential from which all creation arises."

"Just as in any other relationship, you have made a promise to your heart to create and nurture your relationship. If you break this promise by having an affair with the thinking mind, it weakens the trust within the relationship."

You will prevent any weakening of your relationship with your heart by actively tuning in whenever you find damage beginning to occur. The most crucial step towards creating a happy and healthy relationship is your willingness to work at it; your willingness to tune in, to notice your relationship habits and to begin afresh. Remember that the full responsibility for this willingness lies on you.

Your true nature is already giving you everything through the love of your heart. However, you have to reach out to grasp it.

Laughter and play enable you to relax into the way life is and this willingness to work becomes a joy when these aspects are included in the relationship. Humour will help you to break down and resolve any difficulties that you come across. It also builds confidence and trust in your true nature.

FEEL

Loosen up and feel free of the old, rigid ways of thinking and being.

Tune in and take a gentle breath and release any excess tension with each exhalation.

Simply relax.

Allow yourself to lighten up and become creative in viewing things in new ways. Don't wait until your relationship with your heart has already started to show signs of difficulty. If the relationship begins to feel like a burden or a drag instead of a joy, it is time to look at what ideas you have taken from the thinking mind and started to project onto the freedom of your true nature. Your true nature is never any of these projections. It is totally free from being touched by any thoughts.

If you see any projections beginning to occur, make use of the audio support (available from http://www.TrueNatureCentre.com/shortcut-to-inner-peace) and re-read this book. Simply spend time tuning in and resting here as your true nature and you will rapidly rekindle this beautiful love affair with the one heart of your creation.

"The most crucial step towards creating a happy and healthy relationship is your willingness to work at it; your willingness to tune in, to notice your relationship habits and to begin afresh. Remember that the full responsibility for this willingness lies on you."

Relationship Struggle

As mentioned, the negative emotions of fear, doubt and confusion create the internal tug-of-war, which causes pressure, struggle and fight within your system. You then have to drop this internal fight before you can relax back into the one peace that you are.

When you believe that you are involved in the fight, you are unable to prevent your whole system from reacting with defence and attack. This is described further in the "The Body's Unconscious Responses - To Battle or Escape?" section, in *Chapter Six*.

Summarised briefly; when the thinking mind starts to fight to get its way and you believe it and personally identify with it as being your way, stress, resentment and discontentment are created.

As in any relationship, things get bad really fast when your relationship with your heart turns into a power struggle. Usually, this is seen when you begin to externally act out negative characteristics.

If you see this motion of doubt, fear or confusion and these feelings begin to intensify and create internal pressure, fight and defence, it is definitely time to stop and step out of them, tune in to the sound and relax into 'oneness' with your heart.

There may be resistance to this initially, but tuning in at a time like this and seeing the emptiness of these feelings in relation to the solidly-full love and forgiveness of your heart will reap great rewards. By doing this, you will literally weaken the thinking mind's tendency to linger on negative emotions, until it naturally breaks down.

To come into your full potential, you need to be aligned to the one powerful peace that you are and can be right now. It is always available to you and you don't have to wait for rare moments to be aligned to it. You also don't have to wait for someone else to give it to you. Others can only point to what is already within you.

"If the relationship begins to feel like a burden or a drag instead of a joy, it is time to look at what ideas you have taken from the thinking mind and started to project onto the freedom of your true nature."

Hearing the singing in your ears and aligning your full attention to this sound is your direct path to living your true nature in any moment you choose. And this moment always works the best! All else arises naturally when you are aligned in this moment. There are no problems here. Everything just flows in its perfection.

You can put all of your attention into this moment by tuning in to the sound and the 'oneness' of life at any time that you find you haven't been here. Then, the gap between you and the thinking mind allows you the space to make a choice to stay here, focused in this moment, just as it is. In turn, this wonderful relationship will reach out and touch your external relationships with the magic of your beautifully happy heart.

"If you see any projections beginning to occur, make use of the audio support and re-read this book. Simply spend time tuning in and resting here as your true nature and you will rapidly rekindle this beautiful love affair with the one heart of your creation."

Again, Stop Listening to and Believing the Thinking Mind

This wider perspective on life and how it works will show you the down-to-earth reality of creation. The harsh reality is that you are *doing* over the top of the simple and natural happiness that is already here and the doing will not stop until you stop doing it. This doing we are referring to involves listening to the thinking mind, believing it to be true and acting on its instructions.

To begin with, you need to be able to see that you are the one doing it. You will then see that everything you are doing has to stop because it is a result of listening to and believing the thinking mind instead of your heart.

"Hearing the singing in your ears and aligning your full attention to this sound is your direct path to living your true nature in any moment you choose."

Unfortunately, at the beginning you don't fully understand that you are doing anything, because doing is just normal daily living. This misunderstanding is where difficulty may lie, initially.

It is through correcting this mistake and honestly facing up to the fact that you create the obstacles and that you put them in the flow of your life by attending to the thinking mind, that you will stop doing. Again, tuning in to the 'oneness' of your heart will show you this.

You will realise from this new perspective that you are the one who has to leave alone the thinking mind and its interference. You are the only one who can do this. Once you see and accept this truth, it is the beginning of the end.

Now, as you begin to move in life again, you will see when your personality is picked back up and accepted to be true. The more you see this action, the more conscious you become of it and you have the choice to stop it and tune in once more. The mind hates the simplicity of this because you actually have a system that you will progress with. Therefore, the mind may initially create complexity and the illusion that problems and distractions exist.

Any belief in these distractions gives the mind an excuse for you not to stay tuned in to the still-point of the sound and live your freedom. Each time you consciously believe one of these excuses, you weaken yourself significantly. You lessen the grip of your heart's move in your life and instead bring fears, doubts and weakness in its place.

LOOK

If you find this happening, ask yourself:

- Where is the problem right this second?

Asking to see the truth in this moment while staying tuned in and looking at what is happening right now, helps you to see that there is never any problem. Problems are only created by believing the thinking mind. When you are tuned in to the sound, you live in this present moment and no problems can possibly exist. There are only the next actions to make from the obviousness of life.

"The harsh reality is that you are doing over the top of the simple and natural happiness that is already here and the doing will not stop until you stop doing it. This doing we are referring to involves listening to the thinking mind, believing it to be true and acting on its instructions."

You always have the choice to listen to the thinking mind or to tune in to the 'oneness' of creation through the still-point of the sound. Tuning in will always create the space to see that any apparent complexity or distractions are created by listening to the thoughts and are covering the beauty that simply is. These insights bring strength, power and natural happiness into your life as you move within it.

The Workings of The Mind

Living your true nature is opposite to your customary way of living and will stand out as such. As your attention rests with the sound in the powerful peace that you are, it allows you to have a greatly enhanced perspective on how the mind works. This new perspective gives you a deeper understanding of the thinking mind and totally undermines the foundation of your personal identification with this thinking mind. It will also allow you to live with moment-to-moment richness.

By continuing to tune in, the right hemisphere of your brain is awakened and your connection to personally identifying with the thinking mind is broken. Breaking this connection brings your belief in the thinking mind to an end and you will no longer relate your whole life through this identification any more.

The mind is then free to revert to its natural position, as a submissive tool for you to use when it is needed. Your attention and where you place it is key to this breakage.

Clearly, your attention is not your heart. Your attention is just a naturally arising experience of life, as is your body or the tree outside the window. None of these arising experiences require any extra effort from you to continue doing what they do. They are natural.

"You will realise from this new perspective that you are the one who has to leave alone the thinking mind and its interference. You are the only one who can do this. Once you see and accept this truth, it is the beginning of the end."

"You always have the choice to listen to the thinking mind or to tune in to the 'oneness' of creation through the still-point of the sound. Tuning in will always create the space to see that any apparent complexity or distractions are created by listening to the thoughts and are covering the beauty that simply is."

Your attention is the most powerful of these arising experiences and it can be used to help you to learn the 'one' lesson. By consciously taking your attention off your personality, attaching it to the sound and staying tuned in to the 'oneness' of life, you naturally undermine your attachment to the thinking mind. This creates the space for you to directly experience and live in your everyday life, the true love and the never changing, ageless, timeless peace that you are (which rests beneath everything).

As you rest right here, even subtle creations of the thinking mind are seen as they spin out of your heart. Once you see how these mental creations are produced, you will catch them before they become *real* for you and before you believe them to be true. You will see that these creations are always reflections of the same lesson of life; the lesson that you are already the one powerful peace that rests beneath the reflections of life and you can live as this 'one' right now.

This re-training, of where you focus your attention, cannot be done for you. It is your responsibility to stop acting out this motion of personal identification and just stay here tuned in to your true nature, regardless of everything else. Again, only you can do this. Gently come back to the sound repeatedly, whenever you see or feel a motion away from your heart.

As you now know your true nature, ready or not, you are consciously playing the game of life. It is always your move. You have always been playing. But now you move with a clear purpose and you know the rules!

That means you can sit back, relax, enjoy the ride and move with responsibility to live from the natural happiness and 'oneness' of life, in this eternally present moment.

"The mind is then free to revert to its natural position, as a submissive tool for you to use when it is needed. Your attention and where you place it is key to this breakage."

Filtering Out Junk Thoughts

Imagining your system as a computer provides a simple analogy of how flicking the focus of your attention back to the still-point and the sound affects the flow of thoughts.

The thinking mind is like your email system with no spam filter. As a result, you get lots of junk-mail or junk-thoughts. As you begin to tune in to your 'one' heart, you see that all of life is your creation. This powerful insight adds spam filters to your system. Some of the junk-thoughts then naturally get removed before you even have to see them. As you continue to tune in, more spam filters are added and you get even fewer junk-thoughts as you see more of the true love of life.

Sometimes junk-thoughts still get through. However, you will easily see that it is junk and it can be discarded with the click of a mouse or with the flick of your attention back to your true nature. Occasionally, junk-thoughts may slip through the filters and appear like genuine mail. But a quick look at the sender clearly shows you that it's junk and can be ignored.

After a short period of tuning in and living as one with your heart, the only mail that comes through your system is the real mail. These mails or these thoughts have practical information that you need to make your life flow more easily.

During this whole process, you might get a few *Trojan horse* viruses that slip through your system. This happens when you open up a thought in your system by mistake and give it the power of your attention. Then, the thought multiplies and becomes stored on your *hard drive,* where it is listened to and believed to be true.

When a virus of junk-thoughts slips through the filters and loads itself into your system, it is a good time to run a virus scan, *defrag* your hard drive and get back to basics. To do this, re-read this book, listen to the audio support and tune in until your system is free of the virus once more and you are resting in the joy and 'oneness' of your naturally happy heart.

"Once you see how these mental creations are produced, you will catch them before they become real for you and before you believe them to be true."

Your Attention is Limitless

You must never think that your attention is limited. The attention is yours to freely give to whatever you choose.

The power of your attention nurtures whatever you give this power to. In this case, by staying tuned in to the sound, the power of your attention is multiplied by the one power of life. This multiplication brings unimaginably speedy results when you are consistent and clear.

You are always paying attention but it has mostly been focused on the thinking mind. There is no competition between your attention and the thinking mind because your attention isn't needed for the thinking mind to operate. Therefore, you don't have to compete with the thinking mind for your attention.

When you are lazy and allow the power of your attention to do as it has always done, it pulls out of your body and off into the thinking mind, where it separates into the appearances of life. Once your attention is locked into the thoughts, it is out of the body and off with the fairies, flitting all over the universe and no longer in touch with reality. From there, you are open to the pain of taking life personally. You are also open to believing the blame and judgements of this thinking aspect of the mind – about yourself, others and your life.

As hard as this may be to face, you are never a victim. You are always the creator. Until you see exactly how you create your life, by tuning in and staying consciously aware of your actions, you are more likely to act out the victim role. This is because it seems easier to blame others or life, than to accept responsibility for your actions. You pay a huge price of pain and suffering for this internal dishonesty. However, do note that just as easily, you can flick your attention back to the sound and you are free once more. Then, as you stay tuned in to the sound, you are using your attention to its greatest capacity.

"You must never think that your attention is limited. The attention is yours to freely give to whatever you choose."

Creating an Attention Power-pack

You can imagine your focus of attention as a muscle. Since you have identified with the thinking mind for such a long time, you have become lazy and forgotten to use this muscle of your attention. To begin with, this muscle is flabby and weak due to lack of use. There is the potential for a rippling, strong attention power-pack. However, this requires a short period of discipline; a short period of consciously building up the strength in the muscle of your attention.

All it takes is adding a few extra repetitions of tuning in to the sound to your everyday routine and this muscle will grow to the point where it is strong enough to work for itself. All of the energy that you put into strengthening this muscle of your attention by staying tuned in to the sound is logged in its entirety and can never be lost. With enthusiastic commitment, the habit of unconscious personal identification breaks through to consciously living as one with the beauty and joy of your true nature. At that stage, you have permanently gone beyond the dimension of your personality!

If you wish to live as the peace that you are, spend your leisure hours staying tuned in to the sound, melting into your true nature and in sincere gratitude that life is being opened up to you. As you do this, you begin to see how your focus of attention flicks back and forth into the thinking mind. You also see that there is no problem with this motion. If you can see the thinking mind, it is clear that you are not *in* the mind, believing it to be you. Therefore, you can completely relax.

"There is no competition between your attention and the thinking mind because your attention isn't needed for the thinking mind to operate. Therefore, you don't have to compete with the thinking mind for your attention!"

Strengthening the Power-pack of Your Attention

Now is the time to fully experience being tuned in to the sound and anchored as one with your heart. This will kick-start your regime of building this muscle of your attention into a strong, fully-functioning, power-pack.

You are going to close your eyes and tune in to the sound for a moment. You are also going to open up to a greatly enhanced perspective on how the thinking mind works...

TUNE IN

Lie down comfortably. Take a moment to close your eyes, tune in to the sound and live from the beauty of your heart.

Begin by staring straight ahead and gently focusing on the inside of your eyelids. Then, hear the sound and feel where your attention is naturally resting in the lower, middle part of your head.

Now, step out of the mind and see the thoughts and feelings are not who you are.

TUNE IN

Allow the body to relax as your hold on the one package of the person releases. This should *include the natural letting go of any attachment to the sound.*

This simply leaves the back of the eyelids and the sound, in the still-point of peace.

Now, allow yourself to fall back further, sinking deeper into relaxation. Your body is becoming so relaxed, almost at the point of sleep, with just the sound that is still here.

Naturally and simply, let life be, just as it is. There is no need for you to rise up to the superficial mind or to move in any way. Forget everything and simply hear the sound, keeping it as simple as it is.

Still here, with eyes closed, hearing the sound, you will relax and sink deeper and deeper.

Now, stay here...

Ah ah, I said stay here...

Okay. Did you feel the peace at the very beginning? You close your eyes and you see an empty space. You see the inside of the eyelids and nothing more. Within a few moments of staying here, both the mind and your body begin to relax and you simply rest.

At some point, the thinking mind may have something to say, somewhere to go. It knows better. It's bored and therefore creates energetic bodily experiences or whatever else it can come up with. You give the thoughts or the experiences one moment of attention and then, a moment later, you find that you have automatically personally identified with them and have left this place of peace behind.

This one habitual pattern happens through a moment of inattention or rather through the power of your attention automatically and unconsciously being fed into the thinking mind. When your eyes are closed, you will see that this habitual pattern has a slight physical movement. Your eyes move from staring straight ahead at the inside of the eyelids and they flick up to the top right or left-hand side. In this motion of your eyes, you have unconsciously picked up your personality, left your body and disappeared into the thinking mind.

"If you can see the thinking mind, it is clear that you are not in the mind, believing it to be you. Therefore, you can completely relax."

As you see this one habitual motion of picking up your personality identification, it creates the choice for you to either stay here with the sound or to believe this identification with the personality. It is entirely up to you.

Can you guess what your heart would suggest?

From this point on in your life, instead of this motion of personal identification being unconscious and automatic, it is your conscious responsibility to either allow your attention to go out into the creations of the thinking mind and its personality, or not.

This one motion of unconscious personal identification is repeating itself all the way through your life. Consciously aligning to the sound is always an easy key to your freedom from this painful action. If this movement away from the sound and out into the thinking mind and unconscious personal identification wasn't seen this time, it is perfectly fine. Simply tune in to the sound, go back to the start of this section and read it again from the beginning.

The Powerful Peace Meditation and Still-Point audio support will also assist you in strengthening the muscle of your attention.

"As you see this one habitual motion of picking up your personality identification, it creates the choice for you to either stay here with the sound or to believe this identification with the personality. It is entirely up to you."

What You Have Learnt from Chapter Five

This relationship is yours to develop in whatever way works for you. It is a purely intimate affair.

Now, as you build a beautiful, strong relationship with your heart, you can feel the wonder of this healthy relationship much more deeply. This feeling of wonder will bring a profound feeling of gratitude in knowing that your glorious heart is now your best friend in life.

Do your best not to project anything onto your true nature in any way. Your heart is also not an object. It is the sea of potential from which all creation arises.

Just as in any other relationship, you have made a promise to your heart to create and nurture your relationship. If you break this promise by having an affair with the thinking mind, it weakens the trust within the relationship.

The most crucial step towards creating a happy and healthy relationship is your willingness to work at it; your willingness to tune in, to notice your relationship habits and to begin afresh Remember that the full responsibility for this willingness lies on you.

If the relationship begins to feel like a burden or a drag instead of a joy, it is time to look at what ideas you have taken from the thinking mind and started to project onto the freedom of your true nature.

If you see any projections beginning to occur, make use of the audio support and re-read this book. Simply spend time tuning in and resting here as your true nature and you will rapidly rekindle this beautiful love affair with the one heart of your creation.

Hearing the singing in your ears and aligning your full attention to this sound is your direct path to living your true nature in any moment you choose.

The harsh reality is that you are *doing* over the top of the simple and natural happiness that is already here and the doing will not stop until you stop doing it. This doing we are referring to involves listening to the thinking mind, believing it to be true and acting on its instructions.

You will realise from this new perspective that you are the one who has to leave alone the thinking mind and its interference. You are the only one who can do this. Once you see and accept this truth, it is the beginning of the end.

You always have the choice to listen to the thinking mind or to tune in to the 'oneness' of creation through the still-point of the sound. Tuning in will always create the space to see that any apparent complexity or distractions are created by listening to the thoughts and are covering the beauty that simply is.

The mind is then free to revert to its natural position, as a submissive tool for you to use when it is needed. Your attention and where you place it is key to this breakage.

Once you see how these mental creations are produced, you will catch them before they become *real* for you and before you believe them to be true.

You must never think that your attention is limited. The attention is yours to freely give to whatever you choose.

There is no competition between your attention and the thinking mind because your attention isn't needed for the thinking mind to operate. Therefore, you don't have to compete with the thinking mind for your attention!

If you can see the thinking mind, it is clear that you are not *in* the mind, believing it to be you. Therefore, you can completely relax.

As you see this one habitual motion of picking up your personality identification, it creates the choice for you to either stay here with the sound or to believe this identification with the personality. It is entirely up to you.

Chapter Six

The Reflections in Your Mirror

&

This chapter is about how life is constantly reflecting your creation back to you and about seeing how you create things over and over through the habit of believing your thinking mind. However, this chapter mainly points to how by connecting to your true nature, you can change these reflections to harmoniously reflect your relationship with your heart.

In this chapter we will cover:

- The Mirror of Life – Always Judging Yourself through Others

- The Thinking Mind is Incapable of Correct Judgment

- The Body's Unconscious Responses – To Battle or Escape?

- You Have Chosen Your True Nature, So the Struggle Will Stop

- See the Pattern in Your Behaviour

- Seeing and Feeling Deeper into Life

- Accept the Challenge and Do It Now!

- Relaxing into the Way Life Is

- Creating Harmony in Your Life

Now, before you continue tune in and then read on.

The Mirror of Life - Always Judging Yourself through Others

Remember that life truly is a hall of mirrors. It is always your own reflection (the one spinning world in your chest that you hold within you) that you see in your friends, family and acquaintances. As is the within, so is the without.

Any judgements in life, whatsoever, are just an unconscious habit of the thinking mind. These judgements bring that old familiar, internal tug-of-war of fight, struggle and conflict. Any judgements that you believe about others are inevitably reflected straight back to you like a boomerang. So, beware of accepting the thinking mind's judgements of others, lest you be judged.

"This one motion of unconscious personal identification is repeating itself all the way through your life. Consciously aligning to the sound is always an easy key to your freedom from this painful action."

The influence of the thinking mind and its mistaken beliefs that you have accepted as being true are solely responsible for these and other unconscious patterns. These beliefs are what you have unconsciously used to make the choices that have determined your life as you presently know it. All of these reflections are there to teach you the one lesson of life; the lesson that you are this 'one' and you can relax into living the 'oneness' of life in this moment now.

By tuning in and looking at these reflections from the still-point of peace, you will begin to become conscious of these patterns and you will see how these false beliefs from the thinking mind mould and shape your actions and your life. These patterns are happening all the time, just like breathing or the beating of your physical heart.

LOOK

Tune in to the sound and reflect on how the mind's influence makes you act with judgement, anger and agendas.

See how you are now wonderfully free to respond and live differently.

"Remember that life truly is a hall of mirrors. It is always your own reflection (the one spinning world in your chest that you hold within you) that you see in your friends, family and acquaintances. As is the within, so is the without."

The Thinking Mind is Incapable of Correct Judgement

Reliable and true judgement comes from the clear, free mind of the one *overall mind* that is unified and whole, with no personal identification fragmenting and clouding your view.

"Any judgements that you believe about others are inevitably reflected straight back to you like a boomerang."

Never act upon the ideas and judgements of the thinking mind when you are not tuned in to the sound or when you are not living as one with your heart. These judgements are mostly triggered by fear and you will feel them causing tension in your body. When fear is in the mind, mental strength is diffused and you are not capable of clear focus. Stillness, peace, stability and mental relaxation are absolutely essential for effective thinking.

Without living as one with the heart of life, you have an extremely limited and distorted view. This incomplete view is from the perspective of personal identification. Judging your own (or anyone else's) place on this journey is truly impossible from there, as these judgements can only come from the thinking mind. Your true nature would never even look at such things. This journey can only be lived.

Any overt looking to the past or the future is a move away from here; away from this moment and therefore away from your heart. When you personally identify with the thinking mind, it is as if the details you are viewing have been put through a photocopy machine over and over again. With each new copy, the image gets more and more distorted, until you are no longer able to see the original picture.

From this belief in the thinking mind and its creation of the personality, you are only able to see your idea of yourself, others and life in general, through this misrepresentation. As you can now imagine, this limitation distorts the truth, making it totally unrecognisable.

A life that is free of these false judgements brings you to a place of being happy and content with where you are at, now. It brings you to the point where you gladly accept that life can remain the same till eternity. This agenda-free acceptance, naturally detangles your life from any entanglements and opens you up to unlimited possibilities.

The Body's Unconscious Responses - To Battle or Escape?

Potential danger is either from external circumstances or from mental fear. When you are not living your true nature, you are using the thinking mind to judge when you are under attack or in danger. These judgements are often misguided but they still create excessive stress in your system. When the mind creates this stress by thinking fearful thoughts, a bodily reaction called the 'fight or flight' response is activated.

"By tuning in and looking at these reflections from the still-point of peace, you will begin to become conscious of these patterns and you will see how these false beliefs from the thinking mind mould and shape your actions and your life."

This is the body's primitive, unconscious response to get the body ready to battle or escape from perceived attack, threat of injury or threat to its survival. When the 'fight or flight' response is triggered, it changes your system to high alert and everything in your environment is perceived as a possible threat to your survival.

Tuning in to the 'oneness' of your true nature provides a buffer against this stress and will quickly calm down your system when you feel overwhelmed by this survival instinct. When you are tuned in, you won't personally identify with the thoughts or feelings and any stress can then flow out of your system or can simply pass by without touching you. Having this ability to steer clear of this pointless stress leaves your body feeling strong and healthy. As a result, you live longer, achieve more and are naturally happier in your life.

From this one point of freedom and by being tuned in to the peace that you are, you are consciously able to pay attention to the signals of 'fight or flight.' These signals are there to teach you the one lesson of life; the lesson that you are already the one powerful peace that rests beneath the perceived stress of life and you can relax and surrender into living as this 'one' right now.

These survival signals show you that on some level, you are listening to and believing the thinking mind. When you feel these signals arising, it means that you have been living unconsciously. Therefore, you may also need to look and see whether you are actually in physical danger or not!

You may experience physical symptoms of 'fight or flight' as:

- feelings of contraction and tension in your muscles

- palpitations

- sweating

- terror

- rage

- the urge to hit out

- the urge to escape

"Never act upon the ideas and judgements of the thinking mind when you are not tuned in to the sound or when you are not living as one with your heart."

If stress continues, you may experience other symptoms resulting from continued muscle tension and stimulation such as headache, backache, heartburn and stomach ache.

Longer-term symptoms may also be repeating emotions such as feelings of stress, anger, hyper-vigilance, fear, anxiety, depression and becoming tearful. When you experience any of these symptoms, you can use them to remind you to tune in to your true nature and relax and to look at your true, present situation from the still-point of peace. From being tuned in, you can quickly discern whether there is real danger or whether the thinking mind is setting your body up for another false attack.

If there is true danger and you are tuned in as this 'one,' you will be in the perfect position to act quickly and with ease to remove yourself from the situation. If there isn't any real danger, you will avoid an untrue mental attack on your physical system by staying relaxed and tuned in to the sound of life.

Your physical system may have already gone into its defence mode by the time you feel the symptoms. So, when you see this, find a seat or lie down for a moment, remain tuned in and your body will relax and melt into the healing of your heart and the powerful peace that you are.

Recognising the symptoms and signs of being in 'fight or flight' will help you to become aware of when you have left the beauty of your true nature. In the moment of recognition, you can take steps to tune in again and avoid any unnecessary stress. You are then using the energy of 'fight or flight' to help to rewire your automatic responses, rather than to harmfully repeat them again.

"When the 'fight or flight' response is triggered, it changes your system to high alert and everything in your environment is perceived as a possible threat to your survival."

You have Chosen Your True Nature, So the Struggle will Stop

When you choose to live from this 'one' that you are, its light is brought to your life. In the light of your true nature, you will view the impulse behind the actions that you have made in your life. You will see whether these impulses came from the thinking mind or from your true nature. There is no other choice. There is no need to look for these insights. You will be shown everything you need to see as soon as you need to see it.

Through these insights, you will see that when an action is motivated from your true nature, you go with the true flow of life and there is no internal conflict and struggle. During these actions, you will feel the joy, beauty and perfection that flow with the action.

When the mind has set a movement in motion, it can make life hard and it can feel wrong for no particular reason. There is often struggle involved with this motion. This struggle is created by the thinking mind's internal voice or self-talk.

This self-talk is often negative and denigrating to both you and those around you. Somehow, the fact that what was last whispered in your ear was utter nonsense gets forgotten and you automatically believe that this new idea or thought will give you the natural happiness of your true nature. You believe this, even though time and time again, these thoughts work against what you truly want in life.

Again, you can imagine yourself being in an internal tug-of-war. As you become more attuned to your true nature, you will realise that by listening to the thinking mind, you are holding on to both ends of the rope and you are tugging against yourself. This struggle within your system consumes tremendous energy and you achieve nothing by it. Now that you have made the strong and clear intention to stop tugging and to put the rope down, the struggle will stop.

"Recognising the symptoms and signs of being in 'fight or flight' will help you to become aware of when you have left the beauty of your true nature. In the moment of recognition, you can take steps to tune in again and avoid any unnecessary stress."

When you find yourself struggling with life, listen to the Powerful Peace Meditation audio to stop, relax and melt into your true nature.

See the Pattern in Your Behaviour

There is no need to look into the details of the different areas of life and how they are freed from the limitation of personal identification because, as always, the details are not true. The truth of your unconscious behaviour is never in the details. It is always in the overall pattern.

"You will see that when an action is motivated from your true nature, you go with the true flow of life and there is no internal conflict and struggle."

As with the one lesson of life (everything is a reflection of the 'one' that you are), the details are a reflection of the one pattern or the one habit of personal identification with the thinking mind. Simply use the details as a trail to show you this pattern of unconscious behaviour. The pattern that emerges is always to teach you that you have forgotten to live as one with life. Then, you are free to tune in to the sound again. This motion of tuning in to your true nature ripples through the whole matrix of your being, freeing you from pain and suffering created by the mind into natural joy, beauty and 'oneness' with your heart.

Once your perspective has changed by tuning in to the sound, you clearly see how the same mind workings are always at play. You see that it is only the details that change and the one fundamental movement of believing the thinking mind is always the same. With this revelation, you will be free from this one pattern of unconsciously allowing your attention to stay on the thinking mind; free from mistaking the thoughts as being you.

The personality is the gift that holds the secret to this insight. So, you can be truly grateful for the beauty of the personality and for the thinking mind for creating it. Give praise for the treasures that you receive when you no longer personally identify with it. Faith in the perfection of your true nature is enough. With this faith, you will trust that your whole life will be changed for the better.

At times when you find that your attention is once again on thinking, seeing this itself has you free of the mind identification. This is because you see and feel the mind as an object outside of you. At this point, you are conscious and your attention is free to snap back to being tuned in to the sound.

Disease, discomfort and pain are entirely the products of listening to the thinking mind's idea of personal identification. After a while, you will begin to see how you believe that pleasure can be found in the pain of personal identification. Whether this pleasure is from the attention that you get from others or is simply a way of bringing validation to your life is for you to see.

"This motion of tuning in to your true nature ripples through the whole matrix of your being, freeing you from pain and suffering created by the mind into natural joy, beauty and 'oneness' with your heart."

All of the details always boil down to the one core pattern – personal identification. Seeing this pattern gives you the ability to see other people's points of view because you know that you are both the same 'one' with the same core pattern.

When you truly see the pain created by the mind from outside of it, you will no longer be able to identify with it in the same way again. You will see that this pain is completely false and somewhat ridiculous and you will know it is just a twisted and distorted memory from the thinking mind, with no basis in reality whatsoever.

When there is no personal identification clouding the picture, this new perspective of freedom from the pattern of the personality is seen to be always here already. Your heart will show you everything that you need to see for a wider perspective and understanding to be revealed to you.

> "Once your perspective has changed by tuning in to the sound, you clearly see how the same mind workings are always at play.
> You see that it is only the details that change and the one fundamental movement of believing the thinking mind is always the same."

Seeing and Feeling Deeper into Life

If you find yourself falling asleep when you tune in to the sound with your eyes closed, it is alright. It simply shows how relaxed the whole system is and is likely to happen at times. The place just before sleep, where both your body and the mind are at their most relaxed is the sweet-spot. In this place, nothing matters. Your personality has dissolved and the peace that you are now permeates the mind and body system. This is where the rewiring of your life takes place.

It may almost feel as if your attention bounces off the inside of the eyelids and right back into the middle of your brain through to the beyond. You won't need to create this. It will naturally occur whether you notice it or not.

When you tune in to the sound with your eyes open, it may be slightly harder to see the workings of the mind. There may also not be the same physical 'letting go' as you experience with your eyes closed. This is fine too.

You will never lose anything that you have seen during your closed eye sittings. What's more, without your awareness, these realisations are directly translated into your everyday life.

"All of the details always boil down to the one core pattern – personal identification. Seeing this pattern gives you the ability to see other people's points of view because you know that you are both the same 'one' with the same core pattern."

Your true nature is incredibly ordinary, uncomplicated, natural and grounded. This is part of its beauty and charm. Once you realise the fact that your true nature is always here and you stop here, there will be a natural flowering of trust. In the meantime, hold on to staying tuned in to the sound with faith and purpose, living your present life with complete energy and enthusiasm.

The one powerful peace that you are is the source of the universe and therefore, the most powerful element in the universe. It has the ability to dissolve everything that is not true. Your true nature dissolves and dissipates every bit of unconscious personal identification and every wrong condition in the mind, your body and your life. However, as soon as you step into the mind to look, you interrupt the momentum of this process. All you have to do is to get out of the way and let your heart do its work, as you relax and rest in peace.

"Your true nature is incredibly ordinary, uncomplicated, natural and grounded. This is part of its beauty and charm."

Accept the Challenge and Do it Now!

Take Action! Life is as easy or as hard as you make it and your actions define your life. You set the guidelines for your awakening into true living.

TUNE IN & RELAX

Make the choice now to consciously live in awareness in your life and tune in to the sound of your heart.

Relax and use all reminders, all feelings in your body and anything arising in your life to remind you to bring your attention back to the sound and into alignment with your heart.

"The one powerful peace that you are is the source of the universe and therefore, the most powerful element in the universe. It has the ability to dissolve everything that is not true."

As you do this, you will find it becomes increasingly easy to see the thoughts, feelings, speech and actions as they arise. Then, having made these observations, you will move into being consciously responsible by bringing the power of your attention into every situation in life.

Refuse to settle for mediocrity! Jump out of your comfort zone and refuse to accept anything less than the fullness of your heart and you will find yourself moving into a new pattern. This moment is where you will always find your true nature. It cannot be found anywhere else because only this moment is truly alive. In this moment, you are already at the perfect point – the peak of existence. You have simply forgotten this. Now is the time to remember.

If you feel that you have become too comfortable in your beliefs and opinions, stretch and grow. Expand your comfort zone and allow yourself to change and strengthen through trial and error. This is essential for successfully living as one with your true nature.

Love, kindness and acceptance put an end to the internal tug-of-war battle and your external reflection will be a life of peace and joy. It may take a short interval for you to view these changes. However, as you stay tuned into the 'oneness' of your true nature and continue to live in the faith and gratitude that your heart brings, you will find that this positive reflection is created in no time.

As you have read this far, you are bound to build a strong relationship with your heart and receive amazing results in your life. This will profoundly change your life, starting right now! There is no need to focus on bringing about this change. The change simply happens. Like a kettle you keenly watch, it seems to take much longer when you watch it than it does when you leave it alone and focus on living. Therefore, focus solely on the sound and on living from your true nature in this moment.

"Life is as easy or as hard as you make it and your actions define your life. You set the guidelines for your awakening into true living."

Relaxing into the Way Life Is

The key to natural happiness in your life is to embrace and unwind into the way life already is. By staying tuned in to the sound whenever you remember to do so, this happiness becomes your natural way of life.

A set of ear plugs or ear muffs is perfect for the purpose of tuning in. This has been mentioned before, but it is worth reinforcing. Using ear plugs creates a space where the sound will be clearly and fully heard and attuned back to. This attuning is only needed when you continue to overlook the one true beauty of life and accept the creations of the mind that have been layered over the top as being true.

In many cases, thoughts have become overly negative because of the habit of going over the trials and hardships of your day or problems from the past before you go to sleep at night. Lying in bed and thinking about these inaccurate details will make them feel like a big deal and can build a negative perspective on life.

You can weaken this habit by tuning in to the sound and the one powerful peace that you are, while you are in bed at night. When tuned in, you see the positive beauty of your day, regardless of its initial appearance. Give heartfelt thanks for that beauty because you now know that it is there to help you to learn the one lesson of life.

Staying tuned in at night brings peace to your body and the mind. It also creates the space for the natural happiness of your heart to shine through as you fall into a profoundly deep and healing sleep.

You will find that the sound gets louder and more obvious, the more you tune in to it. The ear plugs just need to be used until you find that you are always tuned into unity with your heart. You might like to use them for the first two weeks and then take them off for a few days and see how easy it is to tune in without them. Then you can alternate between using them and taking them off, finding your natural balance.

You do not have to do anything but tune in and melt into the powerful peace that you are. Your attention aligns, your body comes to being deeply at rest, the mind calms, distraction fades away and the sound is all that is here.

"Jump out of your comfort zone and refuse to accept anything less than the fullness of your heart and you will find yourself moving into a new pattern."

Each moment is alive with the perfect response to every situation without the need for thought and when you live in this moment, there is no need to tune in to your true nature. You will already be living it!

Living in this moment restricts any movement to the past or the future. There is no struggle, no trying, no frustration; just the sound.

"This moment is where you will always find your true nature. It cannot be found anywhere else because only this moment is truly alive. In this moment, you are already at the perfect point – the peak of existence. You have simply forgotten this. Now is the time to remember."

Creating Harmony in Your Life

Life is lived for three motives:

- Body

- Mind

- Spirit

Each of these is just as important as the other two. Your heart needs all three through which it lives itself. To come into full harmony in your life, you must have determination to live to your greatest potential in body, mind and spirit. There needs to be a balanced exercise of purpose in these different areas, but without overindulging. If you overindulge in one area, it causes deficiency in the other areas and there will be a natural motion to restore the balance.

Once you have spent a short time concentrating on your spirituality by tuning in to the sound and staying here as this 'one' that you are, balance will be brought into your life. Then these three aspects of life will bring equal interest. There is no need to manipulate how this interest flows, as that motion will be natural.

Simply know that if attention on your spirituality, your body or your mind is taking over, you will intensely feel this imbalance and change will definitely occur to restore balance once more. This change is always good, regardless of the appearance.

From this still-point of your true nature, you have no need to seek or search. You are home, as the natural harmony and powerful peace that rests beneath all movements of life.

"You do not have to do anything but tune in and melt into the powerful peace that you are. Your attention aligns, your body comes to being deeply at rest, the mind calms, distraction fades away and the sound is all that is here."

What You Have Learnt from Chapter Six

This one motion of unconscious personal identification is repeating itself all the way through your life. Consciously aligning to the sound is always an easy key to your freedom from this painful action.

Remember that life truly is a hall of mirrors. It is always your own reflection (the one spinning world in your chest that you hold within you) that you see in your friends, family and acquaintances. As is the within, so is the without.

Any judgements that you believe about others are inevitably reflected straight back to you like a boomerang.

By tuning in and looking at these reflections from the still-point of peace, you will begin to become conscious of these patterns and you will see how these false beliefs from the thinking mind mould and shape your actions and your life.

Never act upon the ideas and judgements of the thinking mind when you are not tuned in to the sound or when you are not living as one with your heart.

When the 'fight or flight' response is triggered, it changes your system to high alert and everything in your environment is perceived as a possible threat to your survival.

Recognising the symptoms and signs of being in 'fight or flight' will help you to become aware of when you have left the beauty of your true nature. In the moment of recognition, you can take steps to tune in again and avoid any unnecessary stress.

You will see that when an action is motivated from your true nature, you go with the true flow of life and there is no internal conflict and struggle.

This motion of tuning in to your true nature ripples through the whole matrix of your being, freeing you from pain and suffering created by the mind into natural joy, beauty and 'oneness' with your heart.

Once your perspective has changed by tuning in to the sound, you clearly see how the same mind workings are always at play. You see that it is only the details that change and the one fundamental movement of believing the thinking mind is always the same.

All of the details always boil down to the one core pattern – personal identification. Seeing this pattern gives you the ability to see other people's points of view because you know that you are both the same 'one' with the same core pattern.

Your true nature is incredibly ordinary, uncomplicated, natural and grounded. This is part of its beauty and charm.

The one powerful peace that you are is the source of the universe and therefore, the most powerful element in the universe. It has the ability to dissolve everything that is not true.

Life is as easy or as hard as you make it and your actions define your life. You set the guidelines for your awakening into true living.

Jump out of your comfort zone and refuse to accept anything less than the fullness of your heart and you will find yourself moving into a new pattern.

This moment is where you will always find your true nature. It cannot be found anywhere else because only this moment is truly alive. In this moment, you are already at the perfect point – the peak of existence. You have simply forgotten this. Now is the time to remember.

You do not have to do anything but tune in and melt into the powerful peace that you are. Your attention aligns, your body comes to being deeply at rest, the mind calms, distraction fades away and the sound is all that is here.

Chapter Seven

The Energy Flow of Creation

In this chapter, you will learn how you create your reality and how by tuning in, you can create more consciously and responsibly. You will also learn how to create more useful and successful habits and attitudes. This chapter will cover:

- Continuous Creation

- An Endless Energy Exchange and the Joy of Giving

- Reaching Out

- Become Sensitive to the Agendas Behind the Actions

- Are You Ready for the Absolute Abundance of Your Heart?

- Fearlessly Facing Life

- What as a Habit? How Are Practical Habits Created?

- Using Your Everyday Habits to Create New, Successful Habits

- Positive and Willing Attitude

- Lifestyle Transformation and Using Time Wisely

- Taking Baby Steps with Dedicated Determination

- Make Time to Devote to Your True Nature

Before you read on, give yourself a gift by tuning in to the sound with your full attention and rest in your heart. This creates openness in your whole being and perfect conditions for real learning.

Continuous Creation

Most people don't realise that their attitude is energy, which is continuously creating results. However, life simply creates whatever you say, think and feel! Because of this, often, the signals you send are not those you intend to send. For instance, life doesn't see any difference between a joke and how you truly feel. So, when you use humour to joke about something in a negative or demeaning way, negativity is being created. This is a misuse of your unlimited power of creation.

You have the natural capability to make things just as you want. Only, you haven't fully realised it yet. For this reason, this capability is misused or rather, used without bringing consciousness and intelligence to it and without using common sense. This misuse happens because the unconscious cannot tell the difference between what is:

- Real

- The overall mind and

- The imagined realities of the thinking mind

This confusion is what creates the belief that you are separated from the 'oneness' of your heart's power. It also creates the belief that you are this person, which you unconsciously act out. You can feel that this belief of being separate from the 'oneness' of life is then lived as if it is true.

Each time you listen to the thinking mind, like it or not, you generate and create something. Every time you step out of the personality package and tune in, you actually stop creating more pain and suffering for yourself (otherwise known as *karma*).

When you bring awareness of this 'oneness' to your everyday living by tuning in to your true nature, the confused unconscious creations will untangle and be brought into balance. These creations will come back into line with reality and into harmony with your heart. Then, the magnificence of the unknown will be the source of your creation.

You have already made the world and everything on it. It is shaped just the way the ideas that you have believed in have made it. There are birds flying above, animals on the surface and insects on and within this beautiful planet. It is awesome in its beauty. This world is a wonderful place and you have a magical gift within you; the gift of creation.

There are many people who, consciously or unconsciously, begin to generate the flow of their creative juices by the power and persistence of their desires. Unfortunately, they often sabotage the creation at the final stages because they are not ready to receive the creation when it comes. By will, your creation is made for you. By being open, you receive it. Whatever your creation is going to be, you must be sure that you are open to receive it.

"Every time you step out of the personality package and tune in, you actually stop creating more pain and suffering for yourself (otherwise known as karma)."

> **FEEL**
>
> Tune in to the sound now and you will find that this 'openness' is already here.
>
> Feel the beauty and depth of this openness as it shines through your body and through your life.

When you tune into the powerful peace that you are and truly know how this life works, joy and happiness spring through your everyday living and all of creation is perfect. Nobody can prevent this perfection from flowing into your life. Only you alone possess this power.

"When you bring awareness of this 'oneness' to your everyday living by tuning in to your true nature, the confused unconscious creations will untangle and be brought into balance."

An Endless Energy Exchange and the Joy of Giving

Life is a wonderful flow of giving and receiving. At all times, there is an energy exchange between you and everything and everyone that you interact with. This energy flow is made by you creating the reflection that you see and then feeling that creation as it is reflected back to you.

When you are closed to either giving or receiving, this energy exchange is disrupted.

There is abundant joy in the act of giving. Giving is as much of a privilege as receiving and for this reason, respect and gratitude towards the recipient are part of the act of giving. Giving is also a natural expression of the awakened heart. Unfortunately, over time, belief in the judgements of the thinking mind has caused a valve to be created. This valve automatically monitors and restricts the amount of giving and receiving that you are open to.

As you tune in to your true nature, you will develop sensitivity to this valve. You will see that you are always giving to and receiving from this 'one' that you are. Therefore, it will become natural to go against the restriction of this valve. With this motion of tuning in to the sound, eventually, the valve will disappear. When you give without expectation, you will then receive with grace and ease.

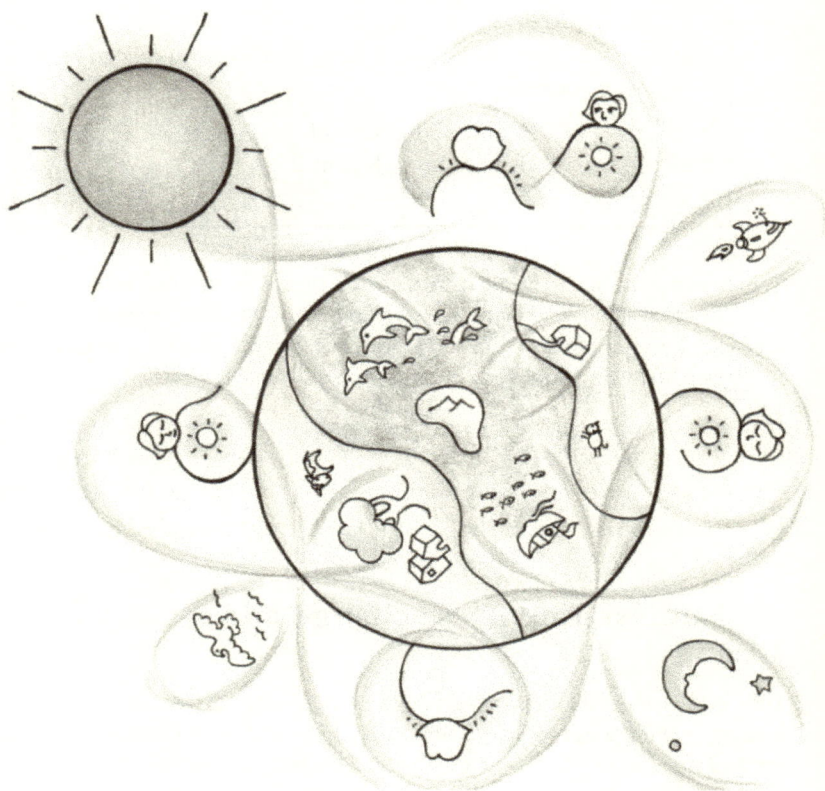

"Life is a wonderful flow of giving and receiving."

As you stay tuned in to your true nature, hoarding and collecting become out of place because you begin to feel how they block this cycle of giving and receiving. When you know that your heart is your limitless supply, this giving becomes a natural expression of life.

Your heart already knows your every need. When you are tuned in and living from the powerful peace that you truly are, you will instinctively know what anyone and anything in life needs. You will know what to give and when.

Now that you know this, you don't have to live with this valve anymore. You already know that whatever you give, you shall receive. So, have faith in this truth and begin to live it as much as you can by tuning in to the sound and living as one with your heart.

Through this open living, you begin to truly understand the flow of giving and receiving from a perspective of experience. This experiential perspective is the birthplace of true wisdom.

"There is abundant joy in the act of giving. Giving is as much of a privilege as receiving and for this reason, respect and gratitude towards the recipient are part of the act of giving."

Reaching Out

A good and easy test for the flow of giving and receiving is *how* you give or receive compliments. If you feel uncomfortable giving a compliment, then you will see that you need some practice in giving. Giving compliments is a great way to bring more 'giving' into your daily life.

The same applies for receiving compliments. When you are given a compliment, notice the thoughts that arise and the bodily reaction in reply to those thoughts. Tune in and use these signs to see any blocks to giving and receiving that you are unconsciously holding onto. By tuning in, these reactive feelings will be seen for what they are and will be free to pass.

Remember that it is always the 'one' lesson that is being forgotten. The 'one' lesson is that you are this one powerful peace that rests beneath the reflections of life and you can live in joy and unity now.

The treasures you receive are precisely relative to the conviction of your attitude, the determination of your intent, the depth of your gratitude and the stability of your faith. If you ever feel that your intent to tune in is faltering, reach out without hesitation and ask for help from your heart or from those around you.

Reaching out for help is just as wonderful for the person you reach out to, as it is for you because it creates an opportunity for you to receive and it also provides the opportunity for that person to give. Generally, people have become so isolated in their own little worlds that both giving and receiving can be difficult, which makes every opportunity golden for everyone concerned.

"Your heart already knows your every need. When you are tuned in and living from the powerful peace that you truly are, you will instinctively know what anyone and anything in life needs. You will know what to give and when."

"Through this open living, you begin to truly understand the flow of giving and receiving from a perspective of experience. This experiential perspective is the birthplace of true wisdom."

Become Sensitive to the Agendas Behind the Actions

The agendas behind the act of giving are often mixed. Generally, there are some that are selfish and some that are selfless. When we avoid facing our own lives, it can become a reason to take an interest in helping other people. Another reason can be the simple need for appreciation.

It is important to become sensitive to the feeling of these hidden agendas, although seeing that there are agendas behind your motion to give should not stop you from giving. As you continue to tune in to the sound, you will develop sensitivity to feeling when the motivation behind your actions is less than pure. Then you can accept whatever the agenda is and create the space for change.

As always, becoming conscious of your actions and why these actions are being made frees you from moving unconsciously in life. This brings awareness to the mind's motivation before these moves are trusted and acted upon. Being aware purifies intention and opens up the opportunity to go beyond the old selfish motion of personal identification to a motion of selfless service.

Continuing to tune in to your true nature will show you very quickly and easily, exactly what you are doing and why you are doing it. By tuning in, you may begin to see some desires that you have to better yourself and your situation. It is perfectly natural to desire to advance and broaden your life. As you see and accept any agendas in these desires, you open the space for these agendas to dissolve.

When you live as one with your heart, any desire comes into harmony with life. The desire is created for improvement for all of humanity, without any feelings of personal gain, competition or jealousy.

When you are aligned with your heart, you cannot even consider yourself alone. You are part of the 'all' of life and any desire is the desire for increase for all. From this one place of peace, you will naturally give more of yourself to those around you. This spontaneous giving shows you that when you do things for someone else, you are making a positive contribution to life. Then, as you stay tuned in to your true nature, the abundance that you feel will overflow to every person you meet.

"The treasures you receive are precisely relative to the conviction of your attitude, the determination of your intent, the depth of your gratitude and the stability of your faith. If you ever feel that your intent to tune in is faltering, reach out without hesitation and ask for help from your heart or from those around you."

Are You Ready for the Absolute Abundance of Your Heart?

There is never the need to try to change anything because any change that happens will be perfect and will happen in its own time. Without manipulating the situations in your life with any agenda, all changes will simply be created by whatever is arising in this moment.

There is no need to exert your willpower on your heart to demand it to give you more. Change will happen naturally when you begin to accept everything in your life, just as it is. In fact, your heart is already giving you all there is. Your heart revels in giving you all that you ever need for the most abundant life you can live.

The question is, "How much will you allow yourself to take of this unlimited supply?"

The measure of your strength isn't revealed by what your heart is willing to give you, but by what you are willing to receive. Your willingness to receive is reflected in your willingness to surrender your hold on the thinking mind and tune in to your true nature because this giving of yourself opens the way for you to receive.

The energy of life is unlimited and is alive through everything! Your true nature is the essence of this life and it seeks to experience itself fully through your body. Therefore, it goes without saying that your heart wants to give absolute abundance to your life so that it can live to its highest potential. You are already receiving this energy to a certain degree. However, you will receive much more when you directly tune in to your true nature and the 'oneness' of life.

Improvement and development are inevitable results of the very act of living. Therefore, it is natural to feel the desire for more, for change and for growth. It is simply evolution. It is the nature of life to continually grow and evolve towards more perfection and ease. By tuning in, you live life to its fullest potential. Life then has no choice but to grow and evolve.

"The measure of your strength isn't revealed by what your heart is willing to give you, but by what you are willing to receive. Your willingness to receive is reflected in your willingness to surrender your hold on the thinking mind and tune in to your true nature because this giving of yourself opens the way for you to receive."

As you live tuned in to your true nature, you will fearlessly face more challenges and through this, more people will be touched by the beauty that only you can offer. This creates a snowball effect, where the momentum is gained for you to experience trust in your heart's move. With this trust, you will be naturally drawn deeper and deeper into living the powerful peace that you are. You will be amazed at what comes to your life in this evolutionary process. The deeper you go, the stronger you become.

Fearlessly Facing Life

Initially, this love affair with your heart will make you face things that you habitually do in your life, which go against your highest good. Your natural quest to live the 'oneness' of life compels you to look at the painful parts of your personality. To become whole and content in your life, you have to face these areas even though it may be difficult.

Don't let any of the insights that you receive by tuning in to the still-point of the sound get you down and don't try to hide from them. If you run away from any feelings or circumstances that you find yourself in, it just drags these feelings or circumstances along with you and they are created over and over again. There is nowhere you can hide from these creations of life. They will always find you. There is no doubt about that!

Often, when looking at the unconscious things that you indulge in, it is easy to get caught in listening to the judgement, blame and denial of the thinking mind. The feelings, emotions and behaviours that are triggered by the thinking mind are all lies, regardless of how justified the mind makes them seem. Nevertheless, it can be seductive to delve deeper and deeper into the details of this behaviour. If you let it, the thinking mind will have you digging until your perspective is so clouded that life looks bleak and depressing and living as one with your heart appears to be impossible.

"Improvement and development are inevitable results of the very act of living. Therefore, it is natural to feel the desire for more, for change and for growth. It is simply evolution."

"It is the nature of life to continually grow and evolve towards more perfection and ease."

You can see the photocopy effect again, where with each copy the image gets more and more distorted until you aren't even able to see what the original picture was. As always, at any point you choose, you can simply step outside of your usual frame of reference and stance of knowing by tuning in to the sound. This will empty the stagnant storage of beliefs and ideas, surrender every bit of knowledge to your heart and allow the one peace that you are to just be here.

In the past, the arising experiences of life were flowing into the body, (through the body) and were held onto. The thinking mind then distorted these experiences and created a disruption in the energy paths of the body. This disruption recreated the same feelings and circumstances over and over again.

When you stop, tune in to your true nature and stay right here, the feelings flow into the body (through the body) and out of the system without any resistance. You surrender to whatever is happening in your life and you experience the *true feeling* that is beneath the appearances.

Once these actions of the thinking mind are seen as reflections of the 'one' single unit of the personality package, they will be openly accepted and set free in one motion. This motion involves tuning in to the sound and melting into the powerful peace that you are. It honestly is as simple as that!

It is truly a gift to see these behaviours and to find that you don't have to act them out anymore. As you begin to grow up and go past these mental pitfalls, you will love the personality just as it is. You will love the personality as a means to see past that personality and to see through to the beautifully natural happiness of your true nature.

Simply notice your world and your feelings. No judgements of good, bad, weak, or strong are to be given any attention. Disregard any intrusive thoughts and just rest as this 'one' that you are. You will then face life fearlessly in the true understanding of how it works and how none of it touches the beauty of you.

"It can be seductive to delve deeper and deeper into the details of this behaviour. If you let it, the thinking mind will have you digging until your perspective is so clouded that life looks bleak and depressing and living as one with your heart appears to be impossible."

"Empty the stagnant storage of beliefs and ideas, surrender every bit of knowledge to your heart and allow the one peace that you are to just be here."

What is A Habit? How Are Practical Habits Created?

To clearly live as your true nature, it is important to know what habits are and how you can use these habits to assist you. In actual fact, everything that you do and think in your life is a habit.

Habits are simply learned behaviour; something that you have done more than once. Before you began to step out of the personality package and tune in to your true nature, each habit was influenced by the one core habit—the habit of listening to the thinking mind and identifying with it as if it is you.

Each belief that you automatically apply to your day, is also a habit. This doesn't make the belief good or bad. It is just what it is; a way that you act with or without conscious thought.

Your daily routines are also habits, although there may be hundreds of little habits that make up the routine. For example, the simple act of getting out of bed in the morning involves many tiny conscious and unconscious habits and decisions. These may be decisions involving:

- What time to get up

- Which muscles to move in the body to get out of bed

- The order that these muscles need to move in for maximum efficiency

- Which slipper goes on which foot

This is where the tool of the overall mind comes in. It is the mind's job to take care of these practical decisions.

When you first learnt to get up out of bed as a child, it took a bit of effort. You consciously worked together with the mind through trial and error to find the best and most easy way of getting out of bed. Once the mind knew what to do, there was no need for any consciousness to be involved in the process. You could trust the mind to tell the body what to do each day to get out of bed. This is an example of the mind in its natural place, doing what it was designed to do. This is exactly how practical decisions have been made into habits. There is no need to bring each of these little habits into consciousness because they are helpful habits.

Most practical habits such as getting out of bed, are helpful and effective habits that work for you. They help to make your day easier by assisting you in performing each task in an efficient and effective way. It is only the unhelpful habits (where you have allowed the thinking mind to have complete sway over the decision) that will fall away by tuning in to the sound and living your true nature.

> "You will love the personality as a means to see past that personality and to see through to the beautifully natural happiness of your true nature."

Using Your Everyday Habits to Create New, Successful Habits

Adding tuning in to your true nature to these everyday habits can be done by using the overall pattern of the habit. When you add a new dimension to a habit such as this, it takes your conscious input just as it did when you originally learnt to get out of bed. It just takes your conscious intention to include your heart in the overall habit and eventually you will be tuning in to your true nature in all tasks of each day.

Once you have started to integrate tuning in to the still-point of the sound in your everyday life, you will successfully replace your old unhelpful habits with new successful habits. This is because you will be bringing conscious daily activity, depth of being and gratitude to your regular, daily habits.

The support audios listed in Appendix Two will also assist you in this process. (Available from http://www.TrueNatureCentre.com/shortcut-to-inner-peace)

The first few weeks of putting these new habits into practice may be slightly difficult at times. During these times, give yourself some pep talks, acknowledging that it will take a short time to retrain a new habit. This will prevent you from pushing yourself too hard.

Be patient; you didn't learn how to read or write in a day or even in a week. Learning a new habit is a process that cannot be rushed. If you try to rush it, you may miss out on crucial lessons and create more work for yourself in the long run.

It doesn't take any effort to work at what you truly want. With tuning in you are fixing your attention on your heart's desire. It is only when you listen to the thinking mind, when it tells you that you want something else or that tuning in is too hard, that you begin to feel that living the powerful peace that you are is becoming a chore.

Remember that every single lesson is a reflection of the same one lesson of life; the lesson that you are already the one powerful peace that rests beneath the reflections of life and you can relax into living as this 'one' right now.

Reach for the extra support audios to stay open, gentle and motivated. You will find that as you continue to enact the new habit of tuning in to your true nature, it becomes easier because you stop listening to the thoughts as if they were true.

You are re-programming yourself to live the one true love and natural happiness of life. You will rapidly find that the benefits of this change of lifestyle have far surpassed the efforts that you have put in. You will systematically improve each area of your life without having to look at one habit at a time because you will be dealing with the one core habit that all other unhelpful habits stem from. This one core habit is always personal identification with the thinking mind.

The closer you are joined to your heart, the more quickly you will receive the power of life in your everyday living. As you tune in, you will find that this closeness will be encouraged and nurtured with your new positive and willing attitude.

"Remember that every single lesson is a reflection of the same one lesson of life; the lesson that you are already the one powerful peace that rests beneath the reflections of life and you can relax into living as this 'one' right now."

Positive and Willing Attitude

When you are willing, the world opens up to you in a way that you could never dream of. Your heart is so full of love for you that it is just waiting for this willing attitude so that it can blossom and share its abundant beauty and joy, just for you. Nothing in your life will change until you change and open up to your heart. This always begins with your attitude. Invite change and commit to it!

Once you are willing to do anything that your heart calls you to do, the road will be smooth and easy. You may still find pockets of unwillingness as you are tested by life but you will be willing to push through and continue tuning in.

Are you willing to do whatever it takes to live from your true nature? Prove to yourself that change is easy because it is! Thinking about change makes it seem hard, if not impossible. How many times have you wanted to shed those extra pounds and thought yourself into not making the effort? This is because of the *'Maybe tomorrow'* excuse. You know very well that tomorrow never comes. So, don't think about it.

Thoughts might arise but don't believe them. Refuse to believe *any* thinking on the subject. In fact, refuse to believe the thinking on any subject. "Just do it!" is a wonderful slogan and when you act in this manner, you will find that it is a wonderful way of life too. Don't try because before long, you will find that you are trying too hard. Remember that you are tuning in to your true nature, back to your natural place of rest and melting into peace. It's easy! Again, don't think about tuning in; instead just do it. Then, stick with it until it becomes part of your everyday behaviour. Always remember, a drop of action is worth a whole ocean of procrastination!

"You will systematically improve each area of your life without having to look at one habit at a time because you will be dealing with the one core habit that all other unhelpful habits stem from. This one core habit is always personal identification with the thinking mind."

Lifestyle Transformation and Using Time Wisely

Please don't just read this manual to experience a nice feeling from its words. Truly experience the natural happiness of your heart and the one powerful peace that you are with the whole matrix of your being by tuning in to the sound. Your lifestyle will transform beyond recognition to being one of ease and joy. This transformation will happen while you maintain healthy relationships, a successful vocation and you live as one with your magnificent heart.

You can be happy right now, no matter what your life looks like. It is a wonderful thing to learn to focus on the beautiful side of life and it is completely possible for you to do so right now. Trust your heart to lead you in this process of remembering the truth of life. All it requires is re-alignment to this moment by forming the right habit of tuning in to the sound and sinking deeply into the relaxation of your body.

There will be revelations and celebrations as you move deeper into 'oneness' with your heart. Your life will evolve into unity instead of disarray and the essence of 'you' will come into its perfect and rightful place.

LOOK

Use this moment to look at your life, as it is now, and see the easy little ways that time can be used to your advantage to tune in to the sound of existence.

For example, if you commute to work, you can use your time wisely. If you drive or walk, you can listen to the audio support and if you take the bus or train, you also have the added choice to read this book and find fresh inspiration.

If you have a 20-minute commute each way to work, that is 173 extra hours per year that you can devote to tuning in to the love of your true nature. Or if you have a 40-minute commute each way, it is about 346 hours per year that you can devote to your true nature, quite easily.

This example shows how every little step rapidly adds up to be a positive force for change.

When you look at the details of your daily life in this way, you will see that there is precious time ready and waiting for you to prioritise and use this time to tune in and be one with your heart. If you don't use this time it inevitably gets wasted in unconscious habits, so re-claim it!

Major breakthroughs can happen in quiet ways as life's circumstances fall into place and what was once a struggle is replaced by easeful being. Expect these breakthroughs when you just do it, now, and tune in.

"Nothing in your life will change until you change and open up to your heart. This always begins with your attitude. Invite change and commit to it!"

Taking Baby Steps with Dedicated Determination

You will learn to live the natural happiness of your true nature by taking baby steps. It always takes small, realistic steps to reach any goal. If you then only focus on each small step, you will find that your confidence becomes stronger and all of a sudden, you have reached the goal with a fraction of the effort that the mind may have been attempting to project.

It takes persistent determination, however, to make this solid habit of tuning in to the still-point of the sound and living your true nature. It is this step-by-step process that is vital and yet, with each step you take, you are enjoying the purity of life. So, don't quit! Continue to tune in until you just stay here.

"Again, don't think about tuning in; instead just do it. Then, stick with it until it becomes part of your everyday behaviour."

"Major breakthroughs can happen in quiet ways as life's
circumstances fall into place and what was once a struggle is
replaced by easeful being."

Tune in again and again, even if you need to do so ten times in ten minutes, even if you may need to do so every ten minutes for ten weeks. It is worth knuckling down and putting your full effort into tuning in straight away. Life is too short to waste by holding back your unlimited potential!

It is perfectly certain that you *will* form the habit of staying tuned in to your true nature if you persevere. Once you have formed this magnificent habit, you will experience a wonderful life that you have never known to be possible.

This sound of silence is the song of life. This song utterly supports and nurtures your union with your heart, helping this union to flower and grow through everything that you touch. This is a straight path to living as 'one,' in the powerful peace that you truly are.

Once this habit is well-formed, it will simply be here without any effort. At some point, you will find that your true nature is naturally integrating into every moment of your day. Take the first step now and begin with this moment.

RELAX & TUNE IN

Stop and relax.

Tune in to the sound of silence that is singing in your ears, and see and feel the motion of your attention as you melt into the beauty of you.

To consciously relate to the power of your heart, your purpose must be to fully live as 'one,' on every plane of your being. Do everything that there is in life for this purpose and it will bring you into harmony.

Be willing and confident because if you follow these instructions, you will know that the life you live is exactly the right life and that it will be perfect. Learn to live so consciously that you will have no work or cares about your home to worry about. This you will do, if you start right now.

"Always remember, a drop of action is worth a whole ocean of
procrastination!"

"It is perfectly certain that you will form the habit of staying tuned in to your true nature if you persevere."

Make Time to Devote to Your True Nature

Schedule a realistic timetable to devote to your true nature. The more consistent you are, the easier it will be to stick to this timetable.

If you initially set a scheduled time at the same time each day and also in the same place and circumstances, it may make it easier for you to stick to your timetable. At the beginning, tuning in can be set up in cycles or blocks of time to preserve the power of your relationship with your heart.

Don't try to completely change your life in one day. It is easy to get motivated and take on too much, creating a pattern that you can't sustain. Gradually nourish, expand and enrich your relationship with your heart until it blossoms into a wonderful friendship.

This is the most powerful relationship you will ever make. Therefore, build it strongly and gently. Don't push it and expect too much, too soon. Gently nurture it and cultivate a deep and meaningful bond. Each day, create the habit of gently strengthening the relationship in creative ways. Become like the tortoise that gently presses ahead until it reaches its goal, rather than the hare that burns itself out by initially overdoing it.

Begin with five minutes today and build it up to ten minutes tomorrow, then fifteen minutes and later, twenty minutes and build on that. Make this a firm routine and refuse to break the routine for any reason.

If there is no time off in your timetable, the thinking mind can come in and project confined and abusive patterns onto your true nature. It is better to build up to a full-time habitual relationship with your heart, gently easing your beautiful heart into your life. This will start a much stronger foundation for you to build on.

There is never any real reason to break this routine of tuning in because your true nature is with you wherever you go. Tuning in can happen wherever you happen to be and with whatever you happen to be doing.

"This sound of silence is the song of life. This song utterly supports and nurtures your union with your heart, helping this union to flower and grow through everything that you touch. This is a straight path to living as 'one,' in the powerful peace that you truly are."

"To consciously relate to the power of your heart, your purpose must be to fully live as 'one,' on every plane of your being. Do everything that there is in life for this purpose and it will bring you into harmony."

REMEMBER

Do you remember what you imprinted onto your mind forever in the Introduction?

That's right:

There is nothing that is more important in life, than living as 'one' with your heart.

Your true nature is all that matters. It is the most important part of your life because it is the one purpose of this life to live in unity with your creation.

The Powerful Peace Meditation audio is separated into five-minute sections that allow you to build up to forty-five minutes per session. And if you wish to do a longer session, you can repeat the audio. This will really help you to strengthen your ability to tune in on a consistent basis.

"Gradually nourish, expand and enrich your relationship with your heart until it blossoms into a wonderful friendship. This is the most powerful relationship you will ever make. Therefore, build it strongly and gently. Don't push it and expect too much, too soon."

Now, you are ready to take an important step towards breaking through the barrier you have built by mistake that prevents your natural happiness. You are going to take responsibility for your creation. To help you break out of the old limited habit of personal identification, let's briefly review how life works.

- There is only 'one.'

- In its essence, life is the one original arising that is formed out of the silence that is before creation; the powerful peace that you are.

- This life is a reflection of the one heart that is within you; the heart of your creation and the reflection of your essence, within creation.

- There is one lesson to learn through this life; the lesson that you are already the one powerful peace that rests beneath the reflections of life and you can relax and melt into living as this 'one' right now.

- There is one habit that you have continued to play out; the habit of forgetting that you are this 'one.' Instead, you have believed that you are the thinking mind and a personality package.

"There is never any real reason to break this routine of tuning in because your true nature is with you wherever you go. Tuning in can happen wherever you happen to be and with whatever you happen to be doing."

What You Have Learnt from Chapter Seven

Every time you step out of the personality package and tune in, you actually stop creating more pain and suffering for yourself (otherwise known as *karma*).

When you bring awareness of this 'oneness' to your everyday living by tuning in to your true nature, the confused unconscious creations will untangle and be brought into balance.

Life is a wonderful flow of giving and receiving.

There is abundant joy in the act of giving. Giving is as much of a privilege as receiving and for this reason, respect and gratitude towards the recipient are part of the act of giving.

Your heart already knows your every need. When you are tuned in and living from the powerful peace that you truly are, you will instinctively know what anyone and anything in life needs. You will know what to give and when.

Through this open living, you begin to truly understand the flow of giving and receiving from a perspective of experience. This experiential perspective is the birthplace of true wisdom.

The treasures you receive are precisely relative to the conviction of your attitude, the determination of your intent, the depth of your gratitude and the stability of your faith. If you ever feel that your intent to tune in is faltering, reach out without hesitation and ask for help from your heart or from those around you.

The measure of your strength isn't revealed by what your heart is willing to give you, but by what you are willing to receive. Your willingness to receive is reflected in your willingness to surrender your hold on the thinking mind and tune in to your true nature because this giving of yourself opens the way for you to receive.

Improvement and development are inevitable results of the very act of living. Therefore, it is natural to feel the desire for more, for change and for growth. It is simply evolution.

It is the nature of life to continually grow and evolve towards more perfection and ease.

It can be seductive to delve deeper and deeper into the details of this behaviour. If you let it, the thinking mind will have you digging until your perspective is so clouded that life looks bleak and depressing and living as one with your heart appears to be impossible.

Empty the stagnant storage of beliefs and ideas, surrender every bit of knowledge to your heart and allow the one peace that you are to just be here.

You will love the personality as a means to see past that personality and to see through to the beautifully natural happiness of your true nature.

Remember that every single lesson is a reflection of the same one lesson of life; the lesson that you are already the one powerful peace that rests beneath the reflections of life and you can relax into living as this 'one' right now.

You will systematically improve each area of your life without having to look at one habit at a time because you will be dealing with the one core habit that all other unhelpful habits stem from. This one core habit is always personal identification with the thinking mind.

Nothing in your life will change until you change and open up to your heart. This always begins with your attitude. Invite change and commit to it!

Just do it!

Again, don't think about tuning in; instead just do it. Then, stick with it until it becomes part of your everyday behaviour.

Always remember, a drop of action is worth a whole ocean of procrastination!

Major breakthroughs can happen in quiet ways as life's circumstances fall into place and what was once a struggle is replaced by easeful being.

It is perfectly certain that you *will* form the habit of staying tuned in to your true nature if you persevere.

This sound of silence is the song of life. This song utterly supports and nurtures your union with your heart, helping this union to flower and grow through everything that you touch. This is a straight path to living as 'one,' in the powerful peace that you truly are.

To consciously relate to the power of your heart, your purpose must be to fully live as 'one,' on every plane of your being. Do everything that there is in life for this purpose and it will bring you into harmony.

Gradually nourish, expand and enrich your relationship with your heart until it blossoms into a wonderful friendship. This is the most powerful relationship you will ever make. Therefore, build it strongly and gently. Don't push it and expect too much, too soon.

There is never any real reason to break this routine of tuning in because your true nature is with you wherever you go. Tuning in can happen wherever you happen to be and with whatever you happen to be doing.

Chapter Eight

Taking Responsibility for Your Creation

This chapter addresses the subject of taking responsibility for what you create in life. Whether you realise it or not, you are constantly creating through your thinking mind and this unconscious creation surrounds you. It is the fabric of your life. By consciously aligning with your true nature you can literally change what you create. This chapter will help you to do just that.

The areas covered by this chapter are:

- Taking Responsibility
- Being Permanently Responsible

That might not seem like much to cover, but this chapter is activity based and will require your whole-hearted participation. You will be guided through much of this by the **Taking Responsibility Audio**.

Through your consciously partaking in this chapter, you can literally change your perception of and your attitude to life!

Taking Responsibility

As you now know, the reflection of life on Earth is your creation and the breath of truth is your true nature. You have given birth to this one creation of life. Therefore, in a very real sense, it is your baby.

You can use this analogy to help you relax into this next section because coming into living as this 'one' that you truly are compels you to accept full responsibility for this creation. Taking responsibility in this manner makes you more conscious of the choices that you make in your life and as a result, you take responsibility for your actions.

Firstly, remember that all of the details of life were created out of the planet Earth that is gently spinning in your chest. This life that you see is a direct reflection of what you hold within you in that spinning world.

"Your true nature is all that matters. It is the most important part of your life because it is the one purpose of this life to live in unity with your creation."

All of it is simply showing you what is within you. Without judgement or choice, life is simply an exact reflection of what is within you. Therefore, it follows that the only way to heal the outside reflection and live in peace is to accept full responsibility for your creation and love it from the inside out. Love the source of creation before it is created, by tuning in to your true nature and loving the one world that is spinning in your chest.

It may be difficult to accept responsibility for both, your life and for what everyone else in your life does or says, but when you have accepted responsibility, you will be open and ready to be responsible enough to be in touch with your true power; the power of creation that is within you.

Please refer to the Taking Responsibility audio for extra guidance through this process. (Available from http://www.TrueNatureCentre.com/shortcut-to-inner-peace)

The fingers of creation are like a rubber glove that has been turned inside out and the fingers are all caught up inside. Until the breath of true love blows through that glove, the fingers are trapped inside and can't reach out and touch life with the unlimited potential that they hold.

You will speed up this process by tuning in to the still-point of the sound and relaxing with your heart. From this powerful place of peace, ask the mind to show you everything you need to see in order for this to be gentle and easeful.

"The only way to heal the outside reflection and live in peace is to accept full responsibility for your creation and love it from the inside out."

TUNE IN & FEEL

Tune in to the sound and come to rest as your true nature. Keep your eyes firmly fixed on the inside of your closed eyelids.

Now, feel the responsibility that you carry for creating your whole world.

Feel that this reflection of life on Earth is your creation. Face it as completely and consciously as you can.

Begin to feel this spinning world in your chest. This world is where all of creation comes from. It comes from your heart; the one source of life.

Feel the one package of your life and embrace it all as one creation.

What do you say when you accept full responsibility for something? That's right; you simply say "I'm sorry."

Silently tell yourself, "I'm sorry."

This statement of "I'm sorry" means that you accept full responsibility for all of creation. Take it all on. It's all you.

"I'm sorry."

You are saying "I'm sorry" to that part of yourself, which created your life as you know it. This opens the space for forgiveness to naturally come to your life and love will blossom.

You're not saying "I'm sorry" from an emotional, guilty or upsetting place; tears may flow but there is no need for tears here.

Simply see and feel the fact that the entirety of creation is your doing.

Feel how the details of life have come out of the Earth within you; the world that you can feel in your chest.

Feel how this one planet that is gently spinning in your chest is the origin and the source of all creation. Feel how you are responsible for all of life.

Again, repeat "I'm sorry."

FEEL

Feel how any wants, desires, cravings and addictions in yourself and others are created from this one Earth in your chest and say "I'm sorry."

Feel how the beauty of nature and the joy of living came from this one world in your chest and repeat "I'm sorry."

All of these details were created out of the planet Earth that is gently spinning in your chest. All of it is simply showing you what is within you.

Feel the responsibility that you carry for creating your entire world.

Take it all on; every last drop of creation is your doing. You have made it all.

See its perfection and also see the limitation that you have created.

You have made it all with the ideas and beliefs that you hold onto and the choices that you make based on these ideas and beliefs.

Just for now, accept that this is a fact and that it is the absolute truth of life. Allow this fact to sink deeply into your being.

Embrace your creation and repeat "I'm sorry."

Apologise for the idea of separation and the veil of falsity that has clouded your vision for so long.

Apologise for the misunderstanding and pain that is caused by this idea of separation.

Apologise for listening to the mind and believing it, rather than listening to the beauty of life.

"I'm sorry."

Feel all of creation as it comes to your mind's eye and breathe it all into the spinning world in your chest. You are breathing it back into the 'oneness' that is within you.

The mind will show you some of the different people, places, things and ideas that are or have been in your life.

ACCEPT

They are not separate from you; they are created as a reflection of the one world that is gently spinning in your chest.

Your friends, your finances, your career, your family, are all a reflection of this 'one' that you can feel glowing in your chest.

Still tuned in with your eyes closed, look into this gently spinning planet and feel each of these areas one at a time.

Let the mind show you what you have created, and regardless of how it appears, repeat "I'm sorry."

Feel how each of these creations has been created out of this one Earth in your chest.

Feel that one world and say "I'm sorry."

Feel this vortex of power that is within you in this spinning world, as it sucks all of these created reflections back into itself.

Feel as all of life as you know it is pulled back into your core to be healed and loved back into the 'oneness' of life.

Breathe it into your chest and repeat "I'm sorry."

Feel how you are this 'one' and say "I'm sorry."

Take full and complete responsibility for all of it.

Breathe out and relax, and repeat "I'm sorry."

The world in your chest is on fire with love for this creation and is taking full responsibility for it.

See each main category of life, one at a time, and feel them become part of the one Earth in your chest.

It's all okay. It's simply being pulled back into this place of peace.

Feel as this gently spinning world sucks all of these creations back into itself.

The person that you think you are is now being entirely sucked out of your creation and back into this 'one' that you truly are; into this vortex of power.

SEE & FEEL

Feel the tentacles of separation as they are set free.

Feel all separation naturally letting go and falling away as it disappears into the vortex in your chest.

Feel this one world in your chest as it gently pulls all of life back into the perfection (which is beyond and before creation) and back into this 'one' that you truly are.

As good as any of it may look, it has still been stunted by your ideas of how it should look. For this, you can say "I'm sorry."

Accept it all and let it wash through you—no barriers, no limits. You are completely open in your submission and surrender.

There is nothing that you are not responsible for. You are responsible for everything that you see, feel, touch, taste and hear.

Everything is to be pulled back into the one Earth in your chest with full responsibility. This is the place where everything came from, so life is simply correcting any parts that are not working for you.

Feel how accepting responsibility for these creations sets them on fire to purify them.

And just rest.

You are surrendering to the heart of life, which is the core of this spinning world in your chest.

This process will take as long as it does. There is no rush or no need to linger over this process. Let it be natural. The mind will show you what you need to see. All you need to do is see it and repeat "I'm sorry."

"Feel how accepting responsibility for these creations sets them on fire to purify them."

There is a good chance that you will not like what you feel and see at first. However, it is important to realise that most of your creations were created unconsciously through your distorted personality; the very same personality that you are not.

The beliefs from the thinking mind that you have taken on and personally identified with have stunted growth in all areas of life. Even the ones that look great are still so limited by the past ideas of the mind.

Once this process has finished and you are gently resting with the sound again, you will find that you will automatically accept responsibility for all of life as you continue living it. As you tune in to your true nature, the motion of tuning in naturally and deeply loves this one world in your chest; loving all of creation in its entirety.

However, first, you must make the solemn promise:

"I am one with life. I love this 'one' and am committed to living its strength, power, love and happiness."

It is understood that you won't be living in immediate perfect union with this promise. However, your intent to make the promise and to uphold it to the best of your ability is what is most important here.

You are only called to do the best that you can in this moment. So, you can tune in and relax and your reflections will naturally realign with your true nature.

"As you tune in to your true nature, the motion of tuning in naturally and deeply loves this one world in your chest; loving all of creation in its entirety."

Permanently Responsible

From now on, you can tune in to the still-point of the sound and call any person, circumstance or thing that you are having difficulty with into your mind's eye. See them and internally speak to them and say "I'm sorry" until you feel sincere; until you feel them moving from your mind's eye into your chest and into your heart.

Feel the person, circumstance, or thing as they are gently being drawn in to melt into the 'oneness' of the Earth in your chest. Then, feel the love of your heart as it burns up the past and any projected future and simply accepts and loves that person or thing just as it is in this moment. In this process, you have accepted responsibility for your creation, forgiveness has spontaneously happened and the love of your heart is replacing the old, with new love and joy.

This process can be done for anything in your life. It will heal relationships, finances, unhealthy habits, your ideas of separation and anything else that you feel resistance to. This healing is deeply profound and is all done within you. You are accepting your creation and loving it into purity.

As often happens when you hold onto anything from the past, whether a grudge or anything else, it is only you who suffers when you refuse to forgive and let it go.

For this process to work, you have to forgive yourself for your creation and if you can't do that, that part of you is still left unhealed and weak. You then see things through this weakness and 'read' into situations as if they are coming from that place. However, when you look from your new perspective of 'oneness,' responsibility and your understanding of how the world works, you bring forgiveness and love to the picture. Then, you have deeply healed and strengthened that part within you.

If there is anything that you still refuse to take responsibility for, you can use the Taking Responsibility audio while looking in a mirror to forgive yourself and maybe get a deeper understanding of how and why things happened as they did.

As always, the how and why are of no real importance, but as you gaze lovingly into your eyes you may or you may not be shown these reasons.

"You are only called to do the best that you can in this moment. So, you can tune in and relax and your reflections will naturally realign with your true nature."

What You Have Learnt from Chapter Eight

Your true nature is all that matters. It is the most important part of your life because it is the one purpose of this life to live in unity with your creation.

The only way to heal the outside reflection and live in peace is to accept full responsibility for your creation and love it from the inside out.

Feel how accepting responsibility for these creations sets them on fire to purify them.

As you tune in to your true nature, the motion of tuning in naturally and deeply loves this one world in your chest; loving all of creation in its entirety.

You are only called to do the best that you can in this moment. So, you can tune in and relax and your reflections will naturally realign with your true nature.

Chapter Nine

More Helpful Hints to Make This Change Easy

In this chapter you will learn how to really focus your newly freed attention on what you truly desire; being your true nature. In this chapter you will cover:

- How You are Feeling

- Double Action Re-Programming

- Creating Bright and Breezy Boundaries

- Anchoring Your Ideal Image

- Stand Firm and Don't Take Your Heart for Granted

- The Leash of Your Attention

- No Beliefs are Needed, Direct Experience is the Only Proof

So, tune into the sound, drop deeply into your heart, relax and let go!

How are You Feeling?

FEEL

Take a moment, now, to feel how you are feeling in your body.

After reading the jaw-dropping information and breaking through into new wisdom and insights in the last chapter, you might be excited, scared, inspired or challenged.

When you come into contact with such a radical change of perspective, you will find both highs and lows flowing through your system. These are always created by the thinking mind and they have nothing whatsoever to do with you. However, they will feel real to you until you begin to truly see through this thinking aspect of the mind.

"When you come into contact with such a radical change of perspective, you will find both highs and lows flowing through your system. These are always created by the thinking mind and they have nothing whatsoever to do with you."

Again, the appearances are often the exact opposite of the reality of a situation and difficulty is no different in this respect. Difficulty can be a sign of deep change. It is often a sign that you are on the right track. However, difficulty isn't necessary. Any apparent difficulty is merely calling you to learn the one lesson, calling you to live from this new perspective, to live these new understandings in your everyday life.

Often, it is when you feel you are 'onto it' or 'just about there,' that the thinking mind quietly slides back into the picture. So, you can be grateful for any difficulties that arise, but do your best not to create more of them.

LOOK

In any situation, if you feel lost or unsure about which way to turn, tune in to the still-point of the sound.

From here, relax and ask yourself:

- What can I learn from this?

- How is this teaching me the one lesson of life?

And, then:

- What would the heart do now?

- If I am connected to the 'all' of life and the one core of me is the one core of life, then all of life comes from me and I am the creator of everything. How does this make me act towards life?

The answer is always very simple.

"I absolutely love it."

Double Action Re-Programming

Tuning in to the still-point of the sound, and learning to live as this 'one' that you are, will require you to put everything you have into this relationship with your heart. This chapter gives you more pointers on how to pursue this labour of love.

Rest assured that whatever you put in will be multiplied a thousand fold. Through this life training system, you re-program both the internal actions and the external actions. This is important because, as already explained; both the internal and external are reflections of the 'oneness' of life.

The internal actions are re-programmed by taking the power of your attention away from the thinking mind, tuning in to the sound and living from the powerful peace that you truly are. The external actions are re-programmed by staying tuned in and becoming conscious of the automatic actions you have been taking in response to the thinking mind.

You are then shown that these actions are being taken because you have forgotten the one lesson of life; the lesson that you are already the one powerful peace that rests beneath the reflections of life and you can relax and surrender into living as this 'one' right now.

Working from both angles by bringing the bright light of your heart to enlighten your life will squeeze out the deceptive ideas of the thinking mind. This takes minimal effort and optimal honesty and is much more rapid and direct than using one approach.

"Often, it is when you feel you are 'onto it' or 'just about there,' that the thinking mind quietly slides back into the picture. So, you can be grateful for any difficulties that arise, but do your best not to create more of them."

Creating Bright and Breezy Boundaries

The best way to stay uplifted and devoted to tuning in to the sound is to keep your life filled with the natural happiness of your true nature. The thinking mind is one-track. It cannot bring up opposite thoughts at the same time.

To outmanoeuvre the thinking mind, simply contemplate on the beauty and power of your true nature by abiding in it, in as many moments as you possibly can. This leaves no room for the mind to play out its ideas. Always start with this moment and stick with *this* moment. Make a commitment to your relationship with your heart and take some time to write down this commitment.

Give the unconscious mind a new set of instructions to live by. For example, it may be that to begin with, you will tune in to the sound before you sleep at night and as you wake up in the morning. Then, build up the time to listen to the Powerful Peace Meditation audio each day and lie down with ear plugs on, twice a day, for thirty minutes. You might also write down that you will tune in as often as you see any movement away from the 'oneness' of your true nature. In this manner, you can establish a new, grounded, habit in your life.

ACTION

Write down:

"These are the steps I will take to integrate the love of my heart into my life."

This is a way of introducing new boundaries that you don't cross and writing down these boundaries makes it easier to commit to them.

Once you have written down these boundaries, you can draw a circle on a piece of paper and inside the circle, write what you choose to create in your life (e.g. joy, peace, love, beauty).

Outside the circle, write down the things that you are ready to release from your life (e.g. pain, suffering, disease, the thinking mind).

When you have finished, cut around the circle with scissors. Cut away all that you no longer choose to create and it will leave only what you 'do' choose.

Re-writing or reading over your list of boundaries, before you go to sleep and immediately upon waking up will reinforce them and help you to integrate them into your daily life. You can also tell the important people in your life what these new boundaries are and explain why you are committed to making these changes.

Explaining the basis for these changes will help your friends and family understand your new behaviour and they can help to support you in your new lifestyle. Your actions may even motivate others to make some positive changes along with you.

Staying within boundaries requires a wonderful new level of self-discipline. It means consciously choosing the people you spend your time with and the activities you spend your time on and sticking to these choices. When you are committed to nurturing your relationship with your heart, any possible obstacles become challenges to learn and grow from. You have decided that:

"I will do whatever it takes!"

"The best way to stay uplifted and devoted to tuning in to the sound is to keep your life filled with the natural happiness of your true nature."

Anchoring Your Ideal Image

Make sure these boundary choices are for your highest good and are helping you reach your highest potential. To help you stay committed to these marvellous new disciplines, you will need to have a clear picture of why living the 'oneness' of your true nature is so important to you.

Understanding that there is only this 'one' and that life is simply reflecting this 'one' to you at all times is a great place to start. This picture will easily be created by direct experience of living as the powerful peace that you truly are. When the mind is busily throwing up thoughts which are going in circles, focus on the sound and experience the benefits of this focus.

FEEL

Tune in and feel the deep bodily relaxation as it flows through every cell of your body.

Feel the deep mental relaxation and experience freedom from any problems and pressures as you merge into the 'oneness' of life.

Deeply feel these benefits as they flood through your system, touching every area of your life.

Consciously feel gratitude for the surrender and complete freedom that these benefits bring.

As you feel these benefits, you are reminded of the positive consequences of bypassing pointless thinking. You will now feel more confident and motivated to remain tuned in.

"To outmanoeuvre the thinking mind, simply contemplate on the beauty and power of your true nature by abiding in it, in as many moments as you possibly can."

In the same way that unconscious living allows the thinking mind to create feelings, conscious living will use feelings to create thinking in the mind. Therefore, whenever you experience doubt or lack of motivation, use the memory of these positive feelings of relaxation, freedom and surrender.

These feelings will remind you and the thinking mind of the benefits of tuning in and living as one with your heart and will encourage perseverance. In this manner, you will deeply remember your picture and stay focused on why living your true nature is so important to you.

> "Feel the deep bodily relaxation as it flows through every cell of your body. Feel the deep mental relaxation and experience freedom from any problems and pressures as you merge into the 'oneness' of life."

Stand Firm and Don't Take Your Heart for Granted

The quality of your relationship with your heart depends solely on how far away you are prepared to be from the joy of living the powerful peace that you truly are. Are you beginning to see the old habits of believing the thinking mind as they draw your focus of attention away from being tuned in?

Instead of simply and consistently staying here in this moment, the thinking mind will do its best to convince you to leave this place. It will also try to convince you into believing that it is more important than living the freedom and 'oneness' of life. Remember, the magic of life is in the beauty of and 'oneness' with your heart!

Once you begin to see that the sound is a gateway to your true nature, a lifestyle of 'practice' can be created out of coming back to it. This can result in you taking your heart for granted and will limit its influence on your life.

Listening to the thinking mind when it tells you that your true nature is always here and that it will *'save your bacon'* whenever you feel like returning to it brings a false belief that it is acceptable to waste time indulging the thinking mind. It is not!

Make tuning in to the sound your one motion in life by using basic, habitual patterns to add a dose of the heart to your everyday routine and create a life of joy. As soon as you clearly see that you don't have to live from a place of pain and suffering, you will tune in to the sound and the door will gently open to the one powerful peace that you are. Natural happiness then floods into your life on a wave of joy, washes over you and reveals your innate love, miraculously uncovering the essential truth of your true nature.

"Are you beginning to see the old habits of believing the thinking mind as they draw your focus of attention away from being tuned in?"

The Leash of Your Attention

Your attention may feel like it is on a long leash at the start. So, when you stop right here with the sound, it may take an extra moment or two before your attention comes *to heel*. Then, as you stay tuned in to the sound, the leash becomes shorter and shorter, until you simply stay with the sound.

As mentioned earlier, from here, you will see the movement away and into the thinking mind and not go there.

The leash of your attention is always connected to the 'oneness' of your true nature and is securely anchored here through the sound. This connection will never be broken.

It is just a matter of asking yourself, "How far away from the one power of your true nature are you willing to be?" This is your choice. Whenever, you see that you are not tuned in, you have this choice to pull the leash of your attention to heel and it will shorten. Tuning in is an easy motion. It is completely natural.

The purpose of tuning in to the sound is to build up the stamina to stay right here, as one with life in this eternal 'now' moment. This creates space for the profound love of your true nature to come to the fore. Once touched upon (by staying tuned in to the sound), this love warmly welcomes, envelops and permeates through your personal identification. This love will then love your personality to death.

No Beliefs are Needed, Direct Experience is the Only Proof

The beauty and simplicity of finding this sound and resting in this moment is that you don't need to believe, stop believing or to drastically change your life as it is now. Don't even believe anything that you have read in this book! It is only through your own direct experience of living your true nature that you will ever learn the one lesson of life.

"The purpose of tuning in to the sound is to build up the stamina to stay right here, as one with life in this eternal 'now' moment. This creates space for the profound love of your true nature to come to the fore."

"It is only through your own direct experience of living your true nature that you will ever learn the one lesson of life."

You also do not have to prematurely reject your present life. As your heart is the core of life, you don't need to believe it. It just is. It doesn't require belief any more than you need to believe that the sun will rise in the morning. The only requirement is to live in feeling contact with it.

FEEL

Tune in now and feel the warmth of your heart as it shines on your face and in your chest, and it cannot be denied.

You simply need to live it.

As you live tuned in to the powerful peace that you are, you are under direct inspiration. You are fearless and confident since you know that it is your heart that does the work. You are anchored in this eternal 'now' moment and the absolute peace of the one source of existence is lived through your body, with no unbalanced thinking mind to tell you how it is or should be. As a result, you will find yourself simply resting in your natural state.

You will never know the extent of what is transcended by staying tuned in to the sound. Thankfully, you don't need to know. Let it suffice to say that mind-made experiences and insights that can divert you away from the true path will not occur.

All genuine insights that are required, however, will come easily and simply. They will be seen and left alone in an open-handed motion. This open-handed motion may need a few fingers to be prised loose at first, just by coming back to the sound as much as possible. Coming back to the sound is especially important at times when your personality doesn't want to.

Again, the motion of your personality is known by its close-fisted, knot in the gut, know-it-all, staunch refusal to let go. However, tuning in to your true nature will have you living in:

- Open embrace

- Empty surrender and

- Acceptance of everything as it is

"Without direct experience, living your freedom is only a thought;
an idea, that hasn't been brought through to your everyday reality
yet."

In essence, the one freedom of your true nature is already here. However, you haven't been living this in your everyday reality. Therefore, you have been left with life as you know it, with no change.

Without direct experience, living your freedom is only a thought; an idea, that hasn't been brought through to your everyday reality yet. You must know that this reality is already here before you come to living it permanently. And the point is to permanently stay here as this 'one.' This is the purpose of this eternal 'now' moment.

Forgetting this one point only prolongs any complications that the mind creates. The thinking mind will say:

- "I know it's always here."

- "It's too easy."

- "I'll tune in to the sound later."

Along with other such nonsense the mind may come up with to prevent ease in your life.

When you disregard the chattering of the mind and gently concentrate on staying right here, the leash on your attention will shorten. The journey is then completed. The more you stop and step outside of your identification with your personality (by staying tuned in to the sound), the easier the arising experiences of life are seen and spontaneously released.

FEEL

Now, let yourself get in touch with the feeling of your heart as you relax and melt back into it.

Rest beneath the arising experiences and feel the balance as it returns to your life.

"The more you stop and step outside of your identification with
your personality (by staying tuned in to the sound), the easier the
arising experiences of life are seen and spontaneously released."

What You Have Learnt from Chapter Nine

When you come into contact with such a radical change of perspective, you will find both highs and lows flowing through your system. These are always created by the thinking mind and they have nothing whatsoever to do with you.

Often, it is when you feel you are 'onto it' or 'just about there,' that the thinking mind quietly slides back into the picture. So, you can be grateful for any difficulties that arise, but do your best not to create more of them.

The best way to stay uplifted and devoted to tuning in to the sound is to keep your life filled with the natural happiness of your true nature.

To outmanoeuvre the thinking mind, simply contemplate on the beauty and power of your true nature by abiding in it, in as many moments as you possibly can.

Feel the deep bodily relaxation as it flows through every cell of your body. Feel the deep mental relaxation and experience freedom from any problems and pressures as you merge into the 'oneness' of life.

Are you beginning to see the old habits of believing the thinking mind as they draw your focus of attention away from being tuned in?

The purpose of tuning in to the sound is to build up the stamina to stay right here, as one with life in this eternal 'now' moment. This creates space for the profound love of your true nature to come to the fore.

It is only through your own direct experience of living your true nature that you will ever learn the one lesson of life.

Without direct experience, living your freedom is only a thought; an idea, that hasn't been brought through to your everyday reality yet.

The more you stop and step outside of your identification with your personality (by staying tuned in to the sound), the easier the arising experiences of life are seen and spontaneously released.

Chapter Ten

A Date to Be Finished

This chapter emphasises that it is your choice how much you put into being your heart. It also gives you more tools to assist you in stabilising as your true nature. In this chapter we will cover:

- Spontaneous Stabilisation

- There is No Comparison – There is No Other

- Give Yourself a Reality Check

- Consciously Aware in Your Everyday Life

- Unwavering Confidence

- Boost Your Sense of Worth

- Your Response is Your Choice

- Catching Your Response

- Rebalancing and Renewing Focus

- The Benefits and Rewards of Exercise

- It is All Completely Natural

Now, tune in, relax and enjoy as you read on.

Spontaneous Stabilisation

With an attitude of love and acceptance, you will come to live from this one place of your true nature. Through your integrity and commitment to staying here, regardless of anything, your attention will spontaneously stabilise here.

Consciously tuning in to the sound doesn't last forever. It is a means to an end. So, give it a time frame. Choose a certain date from which you will be living free from the influence of the thinking mind. Only you can choose this date because only you know when you will be ready to make that final choice to stop listening to the thoughts and believing them to be true. Once you have decided upon this, just stick to it!

Once you have internally set this date and made it clear to yourself, release all ideas about what the result might be. This opens up the space for your heart to give you a life that is out of this world. Now, put in as much effort as you possibly can to stop and step out of the personality package and tune in until that date.

In the meantime, remember that the axiom 'No Pain, No Gain' is not true and be happy with life as it is now. Breakthroughs don't have to be hard. Often, the most profound breakthroughs happen in the most simple and quiet way. However, their effects will change your life forever.

Each moment is already complete without the need for the thinking mind and the false feelings that it creates. This moment is already perfect, with no need for a finger to be lifted to create that perfection.

Once you stop attempting to manipulate the creations of life over the top of its perfection, the beauty of the 'oneness' of life is revealed to you in all its glory. The deepest core of every insight is the one lesson of life. Spontaneous stabilisation happens when you finally see that there is nothing to see and that there is always the 'oneness' of life being reflected to you, like that hall of mirrors which continues to eternity.

It is only your personality that looks for signs of this spontaneous stabilisation and this can trigger the urge to try to manipulate change. No manipulation of life is required. All manipulation is from your personality identification only. This personal identification has to die. Therefore, whenever this 'looking' takes place, it is time to tune in to the sound and melt into the powerful peace that you truly are.

Once spontaneous stabilisation has settled into your life, you will naturally be grounded in this moment. At that point, the sound can still be used to relax into deeper peace. However, there will be no need to make use of the sound in the same way as when it was being used to re-align to your true nature. It will simply be here and you can listen to it for the joy of it.

"Consciously tuning in to the sound doesn't last forever. It is a means to an end."

There is No Comparison – There is No Other

You will live freely once you know that there is only this 'one' and therefore, nothing else to compare yourself to. You will begin to become aware that each human being is made of the same 'oneness' of life that lives everything and everyone. You will stop looking at yourself and others in a comparative manner.

"Once you stop attempting to manipulate the creations of life over the top of its perfection, the beauty of the 'oneness' of life is revealed to you in all its glory."

Each person is a unique expression of the one beauty of life and each has his or her perfect place in the world. The good and the bad are both simply ideas, which have had labels of good and bad attached to them by the thinking mind. Society and the cultures within it have made a group decision on different ideas and the created labels have become *normal*.

From the powerful peace that you are, these ideas become very easy to drop (like a hot potato), because you see that they are empty, dead, thoughts of the past, which are being held onto and fed the power of your attention.

As you stay tuned in to the 'oneness' of your true nature by simply hearing the sound, you disregard the past and the future and lock your attention into this moment alone. This seals the power of your attention into your true essence. The past and future then fall away because as we just mentioned, without your life-giving power, they don't exist.

"Each person is a unique expression of the one beauty of life and each has his or her perfect place in the world."

Give Yourself a Reality Check

As you already know, you are entirely responsible for everything that happens in your life. And you will be truly grateful for this!

Being aware in this moment immediately brings you into being more consciously responsible for what you create. You always have this opportunity of observing and becoming attentive to your actions and the agendas that support these actions. This, in turn, helps you to accept complete responsibility for your life in a natural, easy and joyous way.

'Seeing' is freeing and to live without expectations or specific results is to live the one freedom of your true nature. Your one point of power over your life and what you create is always in this arising moment. You cannot control the past and the future because all past and future moments are not true. They exist only in the thinking mind. You may be able to do some cleaning up of consequences from past moments, but even that can only be done in this current moment.

"'Seeing' is freeing and to live without expectations or specific results is to live the one freedom of your true nature."

Likewise, you cannot control the future by worrying about what will happen or by wanting and hoping for a particular outcome. The only possible way to influence the future (from the 'oneness' of your true nature) is to be focused in this 'now' moment.

Tune in and stay focused in this present moment and you will be set free from any past hurts. You will see this moment as it is. This creates the opportunity to resolve any old feelings that may have newly arisen, without the build-up of the old energy.

The past and the future are like strong cobwebs that keep you trapped in the cocoon of mental activity. When you consistently sweep these cobwebs away and stay seated in this moment, the cocoon has a chance to break down and the butterfly that you truly are will emerge. Only then will you see the truth that has been obscured for so long.

If there doesn't seem to be any change in your life even though you are tuning in to the sound, this is due to hanging onto the thoughts and forgetting the one fundamental lesson of life; the lesson that you are already the one powerful peace that rests beneath the reflections of life and you can relax and live as this 'one' right now. Again, the deepest core of every insight is this one lesson. Listening to the thinking mind makes you forget this lesson. So, if you find that your life isn't changing, give yourself a reality check.

LOOK

Look at your actions in this moment and ask yourself:

- Where is my attention?
- What is important to me right now?

Remember that this forgetting is now just a cycle and it will pass. However, learn from it. Take some time to attune to this 'one' that you are and truly learn that the thinking mind is a lie.

Consciously Aware in Your Everyday Life

Once you have consciously brought awareness to your everyday life, you will live from a point of confidence and joy. This confidence and joy bubbles through your life as you see the unconscious motivations behind your behaviour.

"The only possible way to influence the future (from the 'oneness' of your true nature) is to be focused in this 'now' moment."

By tuning in to the sound, you become consciously aware as you live your life. Conscious awareness in each moment will help you to see and recognise whatever it is that you indulge in. It will also help you to learn the one lesson of life by becoming consciously aware of your thoughts, speech and actions.

To learn this one lesson, you must be open to seeing what the mind is thinking and to experience the feelings that emerge as a reaction to these thoughts. It means hearing what you say (such as gossip, swearing, criticism, complaining and abuse) and how you say it. It also means being open to seeing what you do and how you do it. By doing this, you will see anything that actively sabotages you from reaching your highest potential in life; the simplicity and freedom of living as one with your heart.

In these observations, you see a space between you and your experience of life. This space *is* conscious awareness. This space gives you the opportunity to see where you unconsciously focus your attention. As you look at whatever is arising, you will see that it is not you.

Seeing and feeling this space of conscious awareness will bring a depth of clarity to your life that makes it very easy to drop the false ideas of the thinking mind, to naturally let whatever it is go and to come back into peace.

"By tuning in to the sound, you become consciously aware as you live your life. Conscious awareness in each moment will help you to see and recognise whatever it is that you indulge in. It will also help you to learn the one lesson of life by becoming consciously aware of your thoughts, speech and actions."

Unwavering Confidence

This tuned-in connection to the sound means that you cannot stray very far from the luxurious home of your true nature and that you will never be lost again. Persistently holding your true nature as the one most important thing in your life multiplies your power, restoring confidence, gratitude and joy.

Generally, confidence and self-esteem fluctuate. One day you may be feeling on top of the world and bullet-proof; the next day you may feel down at the bottom of the pile, scared and alone. Often it only takes a simple sour look from your partner, a work colleague or even someone you pass by in the street, to trigger the thinking mind into a cycle of self-doubt and anxiety. This sour look might have been a little bit of indigestion for all you know, but that makes no difference to the thoughts that are immediately believed to be true.

It also makes no difference to the feeling responses, which these thoughts generate and to how these feelings build a life of their own. If these thoughts and feelings are resisted, it means that you are believing them on some level and they will grow and fester, creating more thoughts and feelings to solidify the righteous attitude of the thinking mind.

When you live in conscious connection with your heart, true confidence never fluctuates. You have surrendered to whatever this moment brings, you know who you are and you have complete faith in your abilities. There is no possibility of arrogance or superiority, as these attributes are unbalanced characteristics of personal identification. Living in this conscious connection, you never doubt yourself or the love that life has for you. You will do well because you are already free. Any negative thoughts are seen for what they are and are transcended by simply refusing to give them the power of your attention.

"Seeing and feeling this space of conscious awareness will bring a depth of clarity to your life that makes it very easy to drop the false ideas of the thinking mind, to naturally let whatever it is go and to come back into peace."

Boost Your Sense of Worth

Your true confidence demands that you remove yourself from negative, restrictive and damaging influences as soon as possible. As you see things just as they are, these situations are perceived accurately and you will refuse to continue having them in your life.

Initially, you must arrange your life so that you are not spending too much time with others who deliberately distract you from tuning in to the powerful peace that you are. Sometimes, when a person wishes to make a change in their life, it can make their friends, family and colleagues uneasy.

"Persistently holding your heart as the one most important thing in your life multiplies your power, restoring confidence, gratitude and joy."

It is now your responsibility to put yourself in a position that helps to boost your sense of worth. When you continue to stay tuned in to the sound, this move will be totally natural. You will no longer choose to be in the company of those who wish you anything but your greatest potential.

As you move into tuning into the powerful peace that you are, you may find that people who you have considered as friends may drop out of your life. The change in you may trigger their own fear of change and fear of the unknown (what they don't yet know), which they are often only too pleased to remain blind to. If this happens, however, you will find that new friends who will support and nurture you will then have the space to come into your life.

Wouldn't it be amazing if your friends, family and co-workers simply accepted you as you are and responded to you with support, trust and love? You will create this for yourself as your life comes back into its natural balance.

"It is now your responsibility to put yourself in a position that helps to boost your sense of worth."

Your Response is Your Choice

In the light of your conscious awareness, you will begin to see the one pattern of how the thinking mind responds to the situations or events in your life. If you observe carefully, you will also see that the way the mind responds to any particular situation affects the thinking and feeling that it creates about that situation. This thinking and feeling also affects the way you speak and behave.

If you look even deeper, you will see that the quality of the thinking, feeling, speaking and behaving affects the outcome of the situation and the impact it has on your life. At first, you may just notice these things as you begin to take more conscious responsibility, but as you see this time and again, you will begin to recognise that there is a choice. The choice is always yours!

You can continue living with the belief in the thinking mind if that is what you choose. You don't *have* to live as one with your heart. Your heart has always been right here and you have already lived without a direct relationship with it for this long. Irrespective of what is happening, you can listen to the thinking mind and whatever it says to you or you can focus the power of your attention on the sound and see the true situation just as it is.

In this moment, there is never a problem. Whatever is happening is happening. Your body may be feeling and the mind may be thinking and everything can be accepted, just as it is. When your focus of attention is anchored right here in the 'oneness' of life, you pay no particular attention

175

to the arising experiences of your body and the mind. Any response you make will be from the clarity of the present moment and won't be a mental reaction to whatever is going on.

This doesn't mean that you won't respond in some way. Instead, it means that your response is coming from a totally different place. Your response is coming from the one place that is free from the influence of the thinking mind, free from agenda and free from any attachment to outcomes.

"In this moment there is never a problem. Whatever is happening is happening. Your body may be feeling and the mind may be thinking and everything can be accepted, just as it is."

Catching Your Response

You may not always catch yourself in the act of responding. Sometimes situations or emotions take you by surprise. However, at any time when you suddenly see that you haven't been tuned in to the 'oneness' of your true nature, there is a moment of conscious choice and you can choose to stay right here.

You must be definite in your choice and by that motion, giving attention to the mind and feelings will be brought to a stop, along with any reactivity. Your heart will then bring full acceptance to the situation, including natural compassion and forgiveness for yourself and anyone else who is involved.

Over time, this will bring more gentleness, compassion and empathy into your life and to your actions. You will see that whenever you act in an insensitive way, it is because the unconscious influence of the thinking mind is at play. When you are unconscious, you are at the whim of the thinking mind. When you are consciously aware, the thinking mind has no such power over you!

Use the one power of your heart to bring more light to your daily life. This is your key to living fully and responsibly and you can make this choice at any moment. Living your true nature is like always having the gentle warmth of the sun on your face. This sun lights up your life and keeps you feeling warm and loved.

This present moment is the place of true aliveness and it is always here. This is the place of responsibility, of life, of truth and of freedom. It is the only real place and it is always here, before anything else. It is your choice to move and respond to life from this one place.

As you become more attuned to your true nature, you will forgive yourself for personally identifying with your personality. You will also see that if you refuse to forgive, it is you who suffers. When you see that it has just been ignorance of your true essence that has blinded you to the perfection of life, forgiveness is the natural result.

Once you forgive yourself, this forgiveness will teach you to instinctively forgive others and will heal any situation with ease. The words "I'm sorry" can be said to yourself to initiate this forgiveness. As forgiveness becomes a natural part of your life, any anger and unresolved issues that you have been unconsciously holding onto will be set free.

"When your focus of attention is anchored right here in the 'oneness' of life, you pay no particular attention to the arising experiences of your body and the mind. Any response you make will be from the clarity of the present moment and won't be a mental reaction to whatever is going on."

Rebalancing and Renewing Focus

If you attempt to tune in while the mind is busy and you are physically drained, take ten minutes for a power-nap. Set an alarm if you can, so that you don't over-sleep and wake up groggy. Ten minutes will be just the right amount of time to give your system a helping hand, until you have the space for a proper sleep.

On the other hand, if you are physically full of life and have attempted to tune in to your true nature, only to find the thinking mind going around in circles on a particular topic, then it's time to take five minutes to create a sweat. Physical exercise can reduce the activity of an overactive body or mind or any laziness that you may be feeling. What's more, five minutes is very easy to fit into your busy day.

You can run up the stairs, do some jumping jacks, push-ups, chin-ups, run on the spot or around the block, jump rope or indulge in a dance—anything that brings your body to the point of a light sweat.

When you exercise, make sure that you engage both sides of your brain by doing a few opposite-arm-to-opposite-leg moves; for instance oblique or crossed abdominal sit-ups or opposite-elbow-to-opposite-knee exercises, in either a standing up or lying down position. This stimulates both hemispheres of your brain and breaks up any fixed patterns of thought or any dullness that you may be feeling.

"When you are unconscious, you are at the whim of the thinking mind. When you are consciously aware, the thinking mind has no such power over you!"

You may feel resistance to doing this, but these little exercise sessions blow off the cobwebs and cause a break in the thinking patterns. If you smile, laugh or use a simple affirmation while you are doing the exercise, you will re-wire the circuitry in your brain and create a strong feeling of positivity and happiness. The results of your exercise will also be highly multiplied and you will feel revitalised.

As you exercise, you metabolise any build-up of stress hormones and swap them for natural *'feel good'* endorphins. This restores your body and mind to a calmer, more relaxed state. If you listen to the body when it needs to rest and have a lie-down, it also restores calmness and rejuvenates your system.

With this renewed focus, you have easy access to the natural happiness of your heart and you will find a deeper and more loving connection with the 'oneness' of life.

If you need extra help, check the available audio support in Appendix Two. This support is there to assist you.

> **"If you smile or use a simple affirmation while you are doing the exercise, the results are highly multiplied and you will feel revitalised."**

The Benefits and Rewards of Exercise

It is hard to be or feel positive when you are exhausted, sleep-deprived or physically out of condition. When you feel physically run-down and tired, chances are that you will listen to the thinking mind and your focus shifts to what is not working in your life.

Exercise helps you to feel better because it increases your natural endorphins and helps any stagnant toxins to move swiftly through your system. When you feel good, your thoughts have more clarity and positivity and your perception is more open. This makes it easier for you to put down the tool of the thinking mind and tune in to your true nature.

Every little bit of exercise will help to strengthen your body. A strong body is a good reflection of a strong internal attitude. Exercise also improves energy levels, posture, focus, general health and sleeping habits. As with everything, don't overindulge with exercise. Just gently add it into your day. Refuse to put it off, simply make it part of your routine!

Use what you already do in your everyday life (where you can). For example, walk part of the distance to work and get the bus or train from the next stop along. You can also take the stairs instead of the lift and after a while, you will find that you are able to climb two stairs at a time with much more of a zest for life.

LOOK

Use this moment now to look at your daily routine and find where you can slot in some extra exercise.

Start to strengthen your internal attitude by making your physical body stronger.

Whenever you exercise intensively for twenty minutes or so, make sure that you lie down for a few minutes afterwards. Take this time to tune in to the sound and let your body relax as fully and completely as possible. This helps the body to integrate the benefits of the exercise you have just done and helps it to naturally rejuvenate.

"When you feel physically run-down and tired, chances are that you will listen to the thinking mind and your focus shifts to what is not working in your life."

It is All Completely Natural

As you consistently tune in to the sound, your heart begins to move out and into your life. You will naturally impress others, making them feel that your abundance will rub off on them. You will be giving more of yourself than you take and as you change, your family, your life and your circumstances will change spontaneously. Your true nature is already right here. As you consciously tune in to it, your surroundings will become charged with the true power of peace. This is because the power of life is being continually pushed towards truth.

If you make every conscious act an act of truth, by tuning in to the sound, it must unfailingly follow that every internal and unconscious function will become true. By tuning in, there is no self and therefore no selfishness or deception. Bring staying tuned in to the sound into your routine straight away and with a touch of discipline, the habit of personal identification will be broken. Relish the challenge and do everything in your power to simply ignore the mind!

"When you feel good, your thoughts have more clarity and positivity and your perception is more open. This makes it easier for you to put down the tool of the thinking mind and tune in to your true nature."

Find time to sit quietly and make the space throughout the day to tune in to the sound. By doing so, you will encourage this love and beauty to take over your life swiftly. It is simply life; loving life.

Your true nature is entirely unknown, which makes it especially easy to tell the difference between the lies and the truth. Anything that can be seen or known is *not* you. It can only be a reflection of you. This is wonderful, because you cannot hold the internal attitude of truth for long if you continue to act out the external appearance of this mind-made lie.

To hold this attitude of faith, truth and gratitude, however, you must tune in to the sound as much as you possibly can in your everyday life. Tuning in stops you from acting out the false and perpetuating this falsity in your life.

You have already demonstrated that you are ready for change and are courageous enough to embrace it by making the move to purchase this book and by putting this system into action in your life. As you stably live your true nature, steadily residing here and tuned in to the sound, you will see how life works and find your place in this life. These insights bring both wisdom and maturity.

Wisdom and maturity are the most beneficial gifts that you can receive because these gifts make you truly independent. You will never be dependent on anything from outside of you for happiness again. You have no needs. You are already utterly complete and content. You will enjoy your own company and every relationship that you have becomes a bond of giving, support and encouragement. What's more, you will not find yourself asking for anything in return.

As you live from this relaxed place of peace, it is natural to listen to what people have to say. You will sense and understand where other people are coming from. You will accept everyone just as they are and you will let them be, without hesitation.

"Your true nature is already right here. As you consciously tune in to it, your surroundings will become charged with the true power of peace. This is because the power of life is being continually pushed towards truth."

The most wonderful service to humanity is in your ability to live the powerful peace that you are. Through your perfect expression of true love, others will be able to find inspiration to seek that truth for themselves. This ability will also naturally inspire others to relax and feel more comfortable in your company.

"Bring staying tuned in to the sound into your routine straight away and with a touch of discipline, the habit of personal identification will be broken."

What You Have Learnt from Chapter Ten

Consciously tuning in to the sound doesn't last forever. It is a means to an end.

Once you stop attempting to manipulate the creations of life over the top of its perfection, the beauty of the 'oneness' of life is revealed to you in all its glory.

Each person is a unique expression of the one beauty of life and each has his or her perfect place in the world.

'Seeing' is freeing and to live without expectations or specific results is to live the one freedom of your true nature.

The only possible way to influence the future (from the 'oneness' of your true nature) is to be focused in this 'now' moment.

By tuning in to the sound, you become consciously aware as you live your life. Conscious awareness in each moment will help you to see and recognise whatever it is that you indulge in. It will also help you to learn the one lesson of life by becoming consciously aware of your thoughts, speech and actions.

Seeing and feeling this space of conscious awareness will bring a depth of clarity to your life that makes it very easy to drop the false ideas of the thinking mind, to naturally let whatever it is go and to come back into peace.

Persistently holding your heart as the one most important thing in your life multiplies your power, restoring confidence, gratitude and joy.

It is now your responsibility to put yourself in a position that helps to boost your sense of worth.

In this moment there is never a problem. Whatever is happening is happening. Your body may be feeling and the mind may be thinking and everything can be accepted, just as it is.

When your focus of attention is anchored right here in the 'oneness' of life, you pay no particular attention to the arising experiences of your body and the mind. Any response you make will be from the clarity of the present moment and won't be a mental reaction to whatever is going on.

When you are unconscious, you are at the whim of the thinking mind. When you are consciously aware, the thinking mind has no such power over you!

If you smile or use a simple affirmation while you are doing the exercise, the results are highly multiplied and you will feel revitalised.

When you feel physically run-down and tired, chances are that you will listen to the thinking mind and your focus shifts to what is not working in your life.

When you feel good, your thoughts have more clarity and positivity and your perception is more open. This makes it easier for you to put down the tool of the thinking mind and tune in to your true nature.

Your true nature is already right here. As you consciously tune in to it, your surroundings will become charged with the true power of peace. This is because the power of life is being continually pushed towards truth.

Bring staying tuned in to the sound into your routine straight away and with a touch of discipline, the habit of personal identification will be broken.

Chapter Eleven

You Will Need Enthusiastic Motivation

This chapter focuses on ways to easily integrate this change to living as your true nature. It reminds you of who you really are and of the power of gratitude.

In this chapter you will learn about:

- The Law of Attraction - Magnetic Attraction of Life
- Break Old Patterns Now
- A Healthy Life
- Problem-free Living
- Failure is Only Success in Disguise
- Remember Your Joy
- You are the Infinite Sky
- Natural Gratitude
- Ensure Your Safety and Strength First
- Would You Choose Positive or Negative if You Were in Charge of The Power Supply?
- Faith is Born of Gratitude
- An Ocean of Faith and Gratitude to Swim in

So let's begin this chapter now with a much talked about subject...

The Law of Attraction - Magnetic Attraction of Life

Are you beginning to notice that when you put the full power of your attention into every act, by staying tuned in, irrespective of how ordinary that act may appear, you have made it into a success?

Simply tune in to the sound whenever you remember to do so and your progress towards permanently living your true nature will rapidly strengthen and intensify. The natural laws of life (in this case the law of attraction) obviously also apply to learning to live as one with your heart. Your heart is clear, generous love drawing you deeper into itself; into yourself. This love is the strongest magnetic force in the universe. A law of life is 'Like attracts like,' therefore, each success opens the door for another success.

If you look at the principles of successful manifesting that are so widely available, you will find that they are all totally natural when living your true nature. They also speed up to a phenomenal degree due to the power of your heart.

At times, this focus of your attention may require more concentration than you are willing to give. However, if you let your attention focus on your personality or the thinking mind, the law of attraction kicks in and you will find much more mind-made personal identification in your life. Makes sense, doesn't it?

Focusing on the thinking mind and its personal identification is what you have already been doing. It hasn't worked very well for you now, has it?

There are no coincidences; you think it, feel it and create it, whatever it happens to be. As long as you know this, you can take full responsibility for your actions. Any side-tracking along the way takes you away from this one true purpose.

Therefore, instead of focusing on the thinking mind and whatever it says, simply focus your attention on tuning in to the sound, until you stay right here. Then, you have followed through to where you truly are; you are living the 'one' powerful peace that you are and magnetically attracting more and more success.

"The most wonderful service to humanity is in your ability to live the powerful peace that you are. Through your perfect expression of true love, others will be able to find inspiration to seek that truth for themselves."

Break Old Patterns Now

It may take a short time-lag for some old patterns to be weakened but it is never as long as the mind likes to project. That is a promise!

"There are no coincidences; you think it, feel it and create it, whatever it happens to be. As long as you know this, you can take full responsibility for your actions."

ACTION

If you habitually leave things unfinished, go home and finish something; anything.

This movement will show life that you are willing to change. There is no better way to create confidence in change than by getting things done and seeing how easy change really is.

Reversing your tendencies like this is a very powerful demonstration of your motivation to be true. You will also be giving your subconscious a new direction to learn. With your personal application, great faith and persistent remembrance, lasting peace will come into your life. Remember, you must include both remembrance and action in the equation.

Remembrance without action will leave you standing exactly where you started. You must actually tune in to the sound when you remember to do so. Generally, reaching out for change only happens when the right cycle comes along. Then, an instant hit of gratification, although temporary, is received and it feels as if you are getting somewhere. The cycle moves around to the next distraction and life slowly reverts back to the old patterns.

Another six months or longer goes by and before you know it, the years are speeding by and the joy of living your true nature has been missed yet again. Often, regret will only be felt later in life, where it is seen that the other goals (achieved or not) were completely hollow. Regret weighs heavily on your heart because it is utterly pointless.

Learn from your own mistakes and the mistakes of others. Don't waste any time in distraction or looking to the possibilities of the future. Hold onto this moment, tuned in to the sound and live from your true nature.

If you find that you have relapsed into forgetting to tune in and the attitude of doubt or discontentment appears again, change it instantly. This is entirely possible; it is your choice in every moment.

TUNE IN

Tune in, straighten your posture and bring your faith in the one power of your heart to the fore once more.

Forgetting to tune in to the sound is not a problem. At the point of recognising this forgetting, simply tune in to the sound again and continue with life.

Refuse to believe that you are anything other than completely loved, safe and cared for. You don't need to use your will to force this faith and peace within you. Your heart will attend to this as you give your attention to just staying tuned in to the sound.

"Remembrance without action will leave you standing exactly where you started. You must actually tune in to the sound when you remember to do so."

A Healthy Life

Having faith in your heart brings health and balance into every area of your life. You will become confident that your life is healthy because everything you see and feel will be natural and true.

By tuning in to the sound you will stop having to just think positively and you will begin to live positively without any doubt that your life is going exactly where and how it needs to.

Live truly in faith, tuned in to the sound and the peace that you are. At a certain point, you will notice the changes that have occurred in your life and they will amaze you. It will feel like a miracle has swept your life clean. All it takes is staying tuned in to the sound and directly connecting to your glorious heart.

Cleanliness and organisation are standards that you will find naturally evolving in your life, as you are drawn deeper into 'oneness' with your heart. These qualities are also natural to the easeful flow of the energy of life. Energy stagnates in untidy and dirty spaces. Corners are the worst areas for this trapped energy. Once you begin to firmly stay in this place of your true nature, you will find that your living areas will need to be tidy, neat and clean. Your life will begin to move in that direction also.

"Forgetting to tune in to the sound is not a problem. At the point of recognising this forgetting, simply tune in to the sound again and continue with life."

Problem-free Living

In reality, life is problem-free. It is only wrong information and the built-up fearfulness of your personality, as it kicks in again, that give the appearance that your true nature is in any way scary or problematic. If ideas of anxiety or fear arise and you personally identify with these ideas as being important in any way, you can know it is the mind feeding a story, feeling, desire or some other form of mischief. This one habit of personally identifying with these ideas is all that is covering over the simplicity of existence as it truly is.

Tuning in to the sound will not necessarily make the experiences that are arising disappear. However, you will no longer find yourself identifying with them. This creates the space for you to take the power of your attention away from them, until they run out of steam and fade away.

TUNE IN & RELAX

Simply stop, tune in to the sound again and step out of the personality package. Look at it and see that it is not who you are.

You will drop the tug-of-war rope, and the struggle with life will be finished.

It does not matter how large a problem may seem to be when you look from a distance. If you stay tuned in, you will find that it will disappear as you approach it. If the problem doesn't completely disappear, know that you will be shown a perfect path through it or around it.

Be aware, however, that when belief yields to seeing and feeling (by hearing this sound and resting right here), anything that blocks your growth will fall away. This may cause distress if it is something you have attached value to or identified with, such as something that makes you feel dominant or special in some way. However, be reassured that you cannot lose anything of true value and when you continue to live as one with your heart, any pain will be short-lived.

"Refuse to believe that you are anything other than completely loved, safe and cared for."

The process of returning back to the one powerful peace that you are is totally natural and mostly happens on a subconscious level when tuning in becomes a habit. Submission to the process of tuning in to the happiness of your true nature, through the sound, is the only choice that you need to make.

"You don't need to use your will to force this faith and peace within you. Your heart will attend to this as you give your attention to just staying tuned in to the sound."

Failure is Only Success in Disguise

There is no such thing as failure in life. Any so-called 'failures' are simply lessons for you to see and learn from. Face the lesson, let it go and be done with it.

Again, every lesson is a reflection of the one lesson of life; to remind you that you are one with this life and to live as this 'one' that you are. When you are fully present and attentive in this moment, this lesson becomes obvious to you. Success, on this level, is inevitable when you are tuned in to your true nature. You soon see that there are no mistakes or wrong moves in your life. There is never any right or wrong. Right and wrong are mental constructs of the thinking mind only. Life is in its total perfection to show you this simplicity in action.

You can see, through your relationships, your work and through every interaction in your life, what it is that you are doing, which may be preventing you from staying tuned in and living your true nature. These will be choices that you are unconsciously making, on a moment-to-moment basis, which are not serving you. This space of awareness empowers you to use this understanding of the disruptive patterns in your life to become more and more present and alert.

You will find that you become less inclined to take things personally and you begin to become open to learning what each person has to teach you. This helps you to learn the one lesson of life and be free. Then, old unhealthy patterns in relationships will fall away as a result of this learning.

"The process of returning back to the one powerful peace that you are is totally natural and mostly happens on a subconscious level when tuning in becomes a habit. Submission to the process of tuning in to the happiness of your true nature, through the sound, is the only choice that you need to make."

When you simply feel the faith and gratitude for your life and stay tuned in to your true nature to the best of your ability, every act and expression that flows through you will be effortlessly perfect, free and wholeheartedly loving.

If any discontentment or idea of imperfection enters the thinking mind, take your attention away from it instantly, by tuning in to the sound. This doesn't involve holding any thoughts or feelings back; just see that these ideas are false and gently change your focus of attention. You will then be brought into alignment with the powerful peace that you are. This is true success!

"When you simply feel the faith and gratitude for your life and stay tuned in to your true nature to the best of your ability, every act and expression that flows through you will be effortlessly perfect, free and wholeheartedly loving."

Remember Your Joy

When you are not tuning in to the still-point of the sound and your attention is on the mind and its thoughts or distractions, or when you are anxious or worried about work or home life, you will find it almost impossible to live without rushing. When you are rushing around, you will forget to tune in to your true nature. This 'rushing' is a vicious cycle. The excuse is always "I'll just do this other thing first and then I'll tune in." Never listen to or believe this thought! It is an ambush of the thinking mind. Any excuse is not true. Remember what is important to you; your true nature and make it your priority.

As you begin to strongly live the essence of you, you will find that there is no need for any rush to live your life perfectly. You don't have to fight for life. It is given to you in full abundance, in every moment. Seeing and experiencing this abundance is essential for you.

TUNE IN

Now is the time to tune in and begin to live from this place of peace and joy, in this moment.

As far as everything that is connected with the thinking mind is concerned, you must forget it. On the other hand, in matters connected with your heart, you must unify yourself with them in thought, speech and action, simply by tuning in and living with your delicious heart.

"When you are rushing around, you will forget to tune in to your true nature. This 'rushing' is a vicious cycle. The excuse is always "I'll just do this other thing first and then I'll tune in." Never listen to or believe this thought!"

You Are the Infinite Sky

IMAGINE

Tune in and imagine your personality as a little cloud.

Imagine this cloud as it gently floats in the vast expanse of the infinite sky.

To begin with, you are in the cloud, covered by it, only able to see the cloud. As a result, you think you *are* the cloud. It is only in the moments when you stop, relax, sink and melt deeply into the true love of this moment and allow your old ideas to be set free, that you begin to see there is a sky.

Once you begin to see something is behind, beyond or more accurately, underneath this cloud of your personality, you will step outside the cloud and simply see the cloud for what it is. It's just a little cloud in the vast expanse of sky.

As you become accustomed to being able to see the one infinite sky, you realise that you have had it all wrong; that you actually are this sky and the cloud only arises in you. From this moment of realisation, you understand that you are not trapped or imprisoned by the cloud of your personality in any way. The cloud is just a natural part of the sky floating past. There is no problem with the cloud whatsoever.

Initially, you may spend time forgetting and again remembering that you are not the cloud. Even though you have experienced the freedom and joy of being the sky, out of habit, you plunge back into the cloud and grab hold of it once more. Then you may fluctuate between the old personal identification and the new, true freedom from your personality; your true nature.

This fluctuation only happens until you have had enough of the pain of believing this indecision. At this point, you stop oscillating to and fro and you simply stay here with your happy heart. You will also see that the 'oneness' of life is the only power there truly is. When you remove this power from personal identification, by removing your attention from it, the cloud of your personality is then free to disappear. Without the obstruction of this cloud, your heart will shine its beauty all through your life.

Being free of the cloud of your personality is a dimension that is different from being wrapped up in the cloud. When no personality cloud is in the way of your vision, everything in your life is seen as it truly is. Life is then seen to be a reflection of the one lesson of life and you relax into living the powerful peace and natural happiness of this 'one.'

As mentioned earlier, this freedom from personal identification doesn't leave you acting like an empty robot. In fact, it is quite the contrary. When you stop acting out the mind-made lie of your personality, you begin to truly live the joy of your true nature for the first time.

Natural Gratitude

As we have discussed, there is one intelligent core from which all life and all power emerge. This core is your heart. It is the very essence of life before it takes form. When you stay tuned in to the sound of silence, you will join yourself closely to this core.

"You don't have to fight for life. It is given to you in full abundance, in every moment. Seeing and experiencing this abundance is essential for you."

From this one place of freedom, you will find yourself feeling continuous gratitude. This gratitude keeps you connected with the power of life. This power feeds your inner strength and builds your energy levels, making it easier for your heart to unify in your life.

It is vital to cultivate this habit of gratitude for everything that comes to you, whether the thinking mind perceives it as good or bad. Give thanks continuously and include everything in your gratitude because everything has added to your growth. Life is endlessly helping you to learn the one lesson. It is helping you to learn that you are the one powerful peace that rests beneath the appearances of life and you can relax and melt into this 'one' right now.

Whenever you look at your life, your body or at your personality, stay tuned in and give thanks for the perfection that you are enjoying. Gratitude has a triple effect, reinforcing your faith, negating the thinking mind and bringing you closer to the everlasting love of your heart.

When you consciously feel gratitude, it triggers a feeling response in the body that activates a change in the movement of the thinking mind. This is a wonderful way to speed up the healing of the thinking mind, back to the overall mind. As the body relaxes into gratitude, the thinking mind relaxes with it.

Neither your attention nor the sound is the fullness of your true nature. You are the peace that rests beneath your attention and deeper than the sound; the peace that rests before all of life. Cultivating this new habit of gratitude is a wonderfully life-giving exercise that you can do for yourself. You will find that the 'oneness' of your true nature has everything you will ever need to live the best life you can possibly live. Your true nature is limitless creation. It is up to you to live as the one powerful peace that you are, by staying tuned in to the sound of life.

FEEL

Use this moment now to tune in to the sound and feel this gratitude.

Take a deep, relaxing breath in and out.

Now, feel this spinning world in your chest and sincerely say "Thank you."

Always fall back on gratitude if you feel that you need support. This support is inside of you and if you tap into it, you will never need to look outside of yourself for anything again.

Starting a Daily Journal of Joy and Gratitude will help you to cultivate this habit of gratitude and bring it more fully into your life. Visit here for your free Joy and Gratitude Journal:

http://www.TrueNatureCentre.com/joy-and-gratitude-journal

> **"When you consciously feel gratitude, it triggers a feeling response in the body that activates a change in the movement of the thinking mind. This is a wonderful way to speed up the healing of the thinking mind, back to the overall mind."**

Ensure Your Safety and Strength First

Without having gratitude in your life, a lack of respect for things as they are creeps into the thoughts and they become filled with dissatisfaction. Any belief in these negative thoughts sucks the power out of your life and weakens you immensely.

FEEL

You can feel this weakening right now, simply by consciously thinking a thought about your life with the word *can't* in it.

Feel how potentially weak and useless that thought can make you feel. Negativity literally produces a short circuit and a reversal in the energy system of the body.

Now, think a positive, grateful thought with the word *can* in it. Experience how strong and happy that thought makes you feel.

It is simply a law of life. Like attracts or creates like, in a loop effect. Negative thoughts create negative feelings, which create negative actions. These negative actions create more negative thoughts, which create negative feelings and so on. On the other hand, positive thoughts create positive feelings, which create positive actions. These positive actions create more positive thoughts, which create positive feelings and so on.

194

"Always fall back on gratitude if you feel that you need support. This support is inside of you and if you tap into it, you will never need to look outside of yourself for anything again."

Once you know how this law of life works, you will consciously use the thinking mind to work for you with positive thoughts of gratitude. You can now decide to be happy or sad! Being happy begins with tuning in to the sound and blankly refusing to listen to the thinking mind.

The value of gratitude is not only about what you will get from it for yourself. Gratitude will overflow and touch everything and everyone you come into contact with. The only catch is that you always have to begin with yourself first.

Have you been on an airplane where the flight attendant stands in the aisle and explains the crash procedures? The flight attendant asks the parents to make sure their oxygen is in place before they are able to help their child. This same principle goes for the rest of life. You have to make sure you are safe and secure before you are in a position to offer assistance to anyone else. You can only offer assistance by drawing others back to the point of creation that is within you and within them, because everything comes from the powerful peace of this 'one' that we are.

To begin with, it may look to others like you are being selfish by putting yourself first. However, it will always evolve into selflessness, as you stay tuned in to the still-point of the sound and live as the beauty of this inseparable 'one.'

"You can now decide to be happy or sad! Being happy begins with tuning in to the sound and blankly refusing to listen to the thinking mind."

Would You Choose Positive or Negative if You were in Charge of the Power Supply?

The wonderful news is that you are always in charge of the power supply. In each moment, you have the choice to tune in to the power of your true nature or to let that limitless power leak out into unconsciously creating more negativity for yourself and your life. Gratitude super-charges this power.

There is no place in your life for misery, grumpiness or gloom. Nobody wants to live with these life-sucking energies around them. Regrettably, there is nothing more infectious than crabby complaining. You can catch onto this habit very quickly and become unhappy and miserable in its presence.

A chronic complainer is happy to destroy any joy that he/she finds, literally feeding on this destruction. This joy such a person seeks to destroy will always be in other people's lives, because their own life will be a reflection of their attitude and won't be a pretty sight.

It is not your birthright to be unhappy. In fact, the total opposite is true. Your destiny is to be as one with your naturally happy heart. Choose friends whom you respect and trust; friends who will support and encourage you in whatever you do in your life. Choose carefully! Don't tolerate grumpy people, both for your good and for theirs. If you tolerate negative behaviour around you, this is a sign that this behaviour is acceptable and you are letting that behaviour continue. This doesn't help anyone, including you.

Walk away from situations where complaint is being encouraged, if you have to. Refuse to listen to such nonsense. Definitely don't allow yourself to be seduced into letting the thinking mind get drawn into it or bogged down with it.

All you need to do is simply tune in to the beauty and joy of your true nature and you will be lifted out of that gloom in a short time. Then, you will be the one who is able to smile and be grateful when everything appears to be going wrong, naturally showing everyone around you that you are a strong and positive force of power and a joy to have as a friend.

If you feel that you are stuck with any negative thoughts and feelings, stop and step out of these thoughts and feelings. Look at them and see that they are not who you are. You may also like to exercise for five minutes to shake loose from those old patterns.

Consciously love and accept the thinking mind and the personality as the one single unit that they are and this will help to break through any old patterns of negativity and struggle. Making gratitude a strong part of your life will help to easily create this breakthrough.

"Without having gratitude in your life, a lack of respect for things as they are creeps into the thoughts and they become filled with dissatisfaction."

Faith is Born of Gratitude

Feeling gratitude also creates faith. This faith then produces more and more creativity, which creates more to be grateful for. When you are grateful, you continually expect good things and this expectation becomes faith.

"If you tolerate negative behaviour around you, this is a sign that this behaviour is acceptable and you are letting that behaviour continue."

Every wave of grateful thanksgiving increases your faith. This is essential because truth is unbelievable to the thinking mind. Therefore, you need faith to create change—faith that is beyond belief.

From the place of the 'oneness' of your true nature, you will open the way for conscious creation that is in line with the perfection of life. There will be no mind-made agenda in this creation. Life will be lived from the still-point of peace and creation will be easeful.

Securely staying in this moment, tuning in to the sound and melting into your true nature should all be part of your priority. Once you live from this place of freedom, then every creation will fall into place. Gratitude creates and sustains faith. Faith shows the way and the way is always clear.

Your heart, which knows everything and therefore lives only true love, has perfect faith in every thought that the unified mind creates. This is because when the mind comes into balance, it only thinks authentic, practical thoughts and all thoughts create with clear intent. However, until you live as this 'one,' the mind will stay out of balance and out of control.

From this place of mental instability, creation is unpredictable and often contradictory in its nature. This is simply due to a diffused mental focus, which confuses the process of creation. Only when you are aligned back to the sound, as the peace that you truly are, will this balance and focus return to the mind and your faith will then arouse powerful action in every creation.

"Consciously love and accept the thinking mind and the personality as the one single unit that they are and this will help to break through any old patterns of negativity and struggle."

An Ocean of Faith and Gratitude to Swim in

By faithfully staying tuned in to the sound, you are claiming the health, balance and contentment that are yours. Holding this claim allows the physical beauty to show itself in every area of your life. Your faith then becomes invincible. Faith, without being tuned in to the sound, is not enough. The action of tuning in and having faith, when combined, acts as the bridge over which you pass to the powerful peace that you are. Life must come through you, not to you. Therefore, stay tuned in and you will find that your life is an open channel for your heart to flow through.

"By faithfully staying tuned in to the sound, you are claiming the health, balance and contentment that are yours. Holding this claim allows the physical beauty to show itself in every area of your life. Your faith then becomes invincible."

This power is yours already. Now, you are simply making yourself responsible, ready and open to receive it. Gratitude is a wonderful cycle of creation, which can be easily built into your life. Tuning in to your true nature strengthens your gratitude for the simplicity that is already in your life and creates good fortune wherever you look.

The more constant and consistent your faith and purpose are, the more rapidly you will stabilise and live as this 'one' that you are, because you will make only positive imprints on life. You will not reduce the effect of this positivity by any negative imprints. Silently saying *thank you* is a wonderful way to renew your gratitude.

When you live from your true nature, you live in a limitless ocean of power and this power is used according to your faith. If you simply apply yourself to staying tuned in to this power in the full faith of your heart, it is all yours. The full power of faith is already within you in the spinning world in your chest and can be easily tapped into to draw you back to your truly natural state of peace. This power is pressing upon you from every side.

You will feel and give gratitude and generally love your true nature in complete surrender and with total abandon. This sparks your fundamental love of your heart, which is an extremely powerful force of magnetism. Then, the ideas of the thinking mind become stripped of their false reality very soon.

"Faith, without being tuned in to the sound, is not enough. The action of tuning in and having faith, when combined, acts as the bridge over which you pass to the powerful peace that you are."

Again, a Daily Journal of Joy and Gratitude can assist you to build more gratitude into your life. A free Joy and Gratitude journal can be found at: http://www.TrueNatureCentre.com/joy-and-gratitude-journal

Selflessly give every idea, including the idea of personal identification, over to your heart and ask your true nature to take over your life in its beauty and joy. This leaves a desire-less state of peace. There is not even the desire for the heart because you are already unified with this 'one.'

198

Usually when faith is spoken of, it is to have faith in something that is outside of you. Without specific intent, the faith is not properly grounded. As you now know, it is not possible for anything to exist outside of your heart. Your heart is life. With this new understanding, you will feel full faith and speak to your heart directly, swiftly calling the love of your heart into the forefront of your everyday living.

"Selflessly give every idea, including the idea of personal identification, over to your heart and ask your true nature to take over your life in its beauty and joy."

What You Have Learnt from Chapter Eleven

The most wonderful service to humanity is in your ability to live the powerful peace that you are. Through your perfect expression of true love, others will be able to find inspiration to seek that truth for themselves.

There are no coincidences; you think it, feel it and create it, whatever it happens to be. As long as you know this, you can take full responsibility for your actions.

Remembrance without action will leave you standing exactly where you started. You must actually tune in to the sound when you remember to do so.

Forgetting to tune in to the sound is not a problem. At the point of recognising this forgetting, simply tune in to the sound again and continue with life.

Refuse to believe that you are anything other than completely loved, safe and cared for.

You don't need to use your will to force this faith and peace within you. Your heart will attend to this as you give your attention to just staying tuned in to the sound.

The process of returning back to the one powerful peace that you are is totally natural and mostly happens on a subconscious level when tuning in becomes a habit. Submission to the process of tuning in to the happiness of your true nature, through the sound, is the only choice that you need to make.

When you simply feel the faith and gratitude for your life and stay tuned in to your true nature to the best of your ability, every act and expression that flows through you will be effortlessly perfect, free and wholeheartedly loving.

When you are rushing around, you will forget to tune in to your true nature. This 'rushing' is a vicious cycle. The excuse is always "I'll just do this other thing first and then I'll tune in." Never listen to or believe this thought!

You don't have to fight for life. It is given to you in full abundance, in every moment. Seeing and experiencing this abundance is essential for you.

When you consciously feel gratitude, it triggers a feeling response in the body that activates a change in the movement of the thinking mind. This is a wonderful way to speed up the healing of the thinking mind, back to the overall mind.

Always fall back on gratitude if you feel that you need support. This support is inside of you and if you tap into it, you will never need to look outside of yourself for anything again.

Without having gratitude in your life, a lack of respect for things as they are creeps into the thoughts and they become filled with dissatisfaction.

You can now decide to be happy or sad! Being happy begins with tuning in to the sound and blankly refusing to listen to the thinking mind.

If you tolerate negative behaviour around you, this is a sign that this behaviour is acceptable and you are letting that behaviour continue.

Consciously love and accept the thinking mind and the personality as the one single unit that they are and this will help to break through any old patterns of negativity and struggle.

By faithfully staying tuned in to the sound, you are claiming the health, balance and contentment that are yours. Holding this claim allows the physical beauty to show itself in every area of your life. Your faith then becomes invincible.

Faith, without being tuned in to the sound, is not enough. The action of tuning in and having faith, when combined, acts as the bridge over which you pass to the powerful peace that you are.

Selflessly give every idea, including the idea of personal identification, over to your heart and ask your true nature to take over your life in its beauty and joy.

Chapter Twelve

A Life of Powerful Peace

This chapter really helps you to hone your ability to live as your true nature. In particular, it focuses on overcoming apparent obstacles to living this life freely. The more you face into these difficulties and keep tuning in, no matter what is occurring and despite the thinking mind's commentary, the stronger, more free and more peaceful you will find your life as your heart becomes. In this chapter you will learn about:

- Creating New Opportunities

- Change of Direction

- Overcoming Adversity

- Cycles of Resistance and Release

- Your True Nature is Worth Every Ounce of Effort

- Shelter from the Storms of Life

- Softening into Your True Nature

- Profound Silence

Since this is again a shorter chapter, take every opportunity that you can to relax into the powerful peace of your true nature whilst you read. Remember, any energy that you put into aligning with your heart will always pay enormous dividends!

Creating New Opportunities

You have already made up your mind. You have created the thinking mind and have fed it with your attention to keep it alive. Now, you can make up your mind to stop making up your mind. You can stop creating the thinking mind because the thinking mind doesn't exist without you. Instead, you can use the 'oneness' of your heart as your compass to draw you home to the truth.

In your everyday life, whenever you see that you have picked up the rope of fight or struggle with the way things are, tune in to the sound. Whenever the package of your personality really doesn't feel like it, tune in to the sound.

Any apparently negative arising experiences are ideal openings for you to strengthen this new habit of tuning in. Not only will you be more quickly relieved of the experience, but also you will literally be breaking through major energetic blockages of personal identification.

Working against your personality identification at every opportunity is the quickest way for your personality to lose its apparent hold. Make staying tuned in a priority in your life and you will not be disappointed. On the contrary; peace, beauty and joy will infuse your being and your very existence.

As you stop the momentum of personal identification in its tracks (by tuning in to the sound), opportunities will come to you in increasing number. Don't be fooled by the surface appearance of the opportunity. Some may present themselves in a negative disguise!

When these opportunities appear, you will need to be very firm in your faith and intention, keeping in close 'feeling' contact with your heart and in gratitude. Simply say a silent 'Thank you' for the endless beauty of life and listen to your heart's guidance. There is never any lack of opportunity when you live from your true nature. A world of opportunity is opened up to you in each moment.

"You can stop creating the thinking mind because the thinking mind doesn't exist without you. Instead, you can use the 'oneness' of your heart as your compass to draw you home to the truth."

Change of Direction

A completely new direction is only possible in your life once the momentum of personal identification has run out through lack of use. When you give your whole heart, body and mind to staying tuned in to the sound, your entire system will change. Staying tuned in, brings freedom and space for the 'oneness' of life to gain its own momentum.

Don't listen to the mind's questions on how you will overcome any problems that may appear on the horizon. By staying tuned in and as one with your true nature, you will clearly see if your direction in life needs to be changed in any way. You will see the perfect moves to make, to create the space for any changes that are needed.

When you set an internal declaration of high spiritual truth, you challenge the old beliefs that are in the unconscious mind. The false is revealed to be seen, felt and allowed to be naturally set free from being held in your system. This appearance of conflict provides the opportunity for growth. It ultimately strengthens the bond with your heart. These conflicts are inevitable because they are already trapped in your system and they need to be set free. Simply seeing these conflicts from the still-point of peace allows them to be released. Therefore, learning to face these conflicts, rather than avoiding them, is crucial.

During times of growth and change, as in puberty, it feels as if your world has been turned upside down. In this case, the built-up dregs of your personality identification get stirred up so that they are seen and discarded from the one point of true love. This happens naturally. Therefore, you can relax and let it be just as it is, allowing these dregs to pass easily out of your system. Throughout these times of change, tune in to the sound and live your true nature, consistently expressing the joy and gratitude that you already are. Be truly grateful that the peace that you are is already true of you. The perfection of life is already yours, simply waiting for your recognition.

"Keep in close 'feeling' contact with your heart and in gratitude. Simply say a silent 'Thank you' for the endless beauty of life and listen to your heart's guidance."

Overcoming Adversity

Often, just before any immense success, there is apparent disappointment and opposition. This is a testing time.

The test is:

Will you go back to believing the dishonest appearances of life?

or

Will you continue to tune in to the sound and rest in the peace that you truly are?

It is always as simple as this. Renew your gratitude and this will bring you back on course, as you tune in to the sound and rest in the power of peace. There is really no choice in any of it but if you struggle with the way life is, it tends to alter your course back to the old ways. This is simply due to faltering faith.

When you hold onto your intent to live the magnificence of your true nature with full faith in its 'oneness,' the beauty of life is revealed. Again, simply saying a silent *'Thank you'* helps the feelings of gratitude to bubble to the surface once more.

"When you set an internal declaration of high spiritual truth, you challenge the old beliefs that are in the unconscious mind. The false is revealed to be seen, felt and allowed to be naturally set free from being held in your system."

When you have made your intent clear to the universe, by staying tuned in to your true nature, you must be ready for surprises. You must also be ready for mistaken appearances. Stand firm, knowing that the appearances are not true. Your life may seem to be heading in the wrong direction, when in reality it is perfectly on course.

You are already perfect. Your perfection has merely been temporarily forgotten. Doubts and fears that the mind conjures up pollute your body. If you believe in what these doubts and fears say and you don't tune in to the sound, it further stokes the fire of the thinking mind, allowing the mind to run riot. There is no need to let this happen. However, if it does, at any stage you can simply return to the sound once more. *Now*, is always good!

There is no need to beat yourself up if you go off on a tangent into believing the mind. Again, there are no failures.

TUNE IN & RELAX

Simply bring yourself back to the peace that you are, by tuning in, and without judgement observe how the thinking mind has tricked you into believing it.

Use this observation to help you avoid falling into that trap again.

After any such incident, it may take a few extra moments to relax back into the power of peace. However, stay with the sound and allow your whole system to re-align to your true nature. It is never too late to tune in to the still-point of the sound. 'Now' is always the perfect time to tune in again and you are free, standing in your one true essence.

"The appearance of conflict provides the opportunity for growth. It ultimately strengthens the bond with your heart. These conflicts are inevitable because they are already trapped in your system and they need to be set free."

"Renew your gratitude and this will bring you back on course, as you tune in to the sound and rest in the power of peace."

Cycles of Resistance and Release

'Letting go' is a completely natural motion. As you relax into 'oneness' with your heart, you naturally let go of your death-like grip on life. This grip has been strangling the natural beauty of life and is holding everything that you refuse to accept, in place.

Wanting life to change produces more want, rather than producing change. This is because want is a belief in lack rather than an abundant and accepting attitude. When you naturally let go of the idea of wanting to change any of the internal or external appearances of life, any resistance falls away and you accept life as it is right now.

Therefore, when you feel resistance and fight with the way life is, welcome it instead. In welcoming any resistance, you welcome the natural flow of life and allow the resistance to be set free. Let whatever it is to just be here, regardless of how it appears.

The flow of life only becomes blocked when you listen to the thinking mind and act on its advice. Believing the mind in this manner causes the mental activity to build. As a result, manipulation, reasons, excuses, blame and whatever else the thinking mind can come up with to fight and control your life, begin to increase.

This is then reflected to you by the arising experiences of life appearing to build and increase, until it seems as if there needs to be a major breakthrough for the flow to return to balance. This is a painful way through life, but unfortunately most people live in this manner on a daily basis. This insanity is called *normal*.

As your body has a certain amount of residual mental binding riddled through it, you may find that it goes through cycles of becoming drained and tired as this binding releases. So, be gentle in nurturing your body, getting as much sleep and relaxation time as possible. These cycles will pass.

If at any time you feel pain, either physical or emotional, it is again time to tune in to the sound, exercising gratitude and faith. Be thankful for the power of peace, which is beneath the pain, and be clear that the waves of pain will cease as soon as your body is ready.

"It is never too late to tune in to the still-point of the sound. 'Now' is always the perfect time to tune in again and you are free, standing in your one true essence."

Your body uses pain to bring your attention to energy that is trapped in your body's system. This energy needs for you to feel it and acknowledge it, and then it is free to pass through and out of the system. Fix your will power on staying tuned in to the sound and living your true nature. Be confident that this heart, which is within you, will bring any trapped pain to the surface to be healed. Once you are attuned to the peace that you are, you will be surprised to find how quickly pain dissolves. You will stop holding on to pain and allow it to naturally come and go.

"In welcoming any resistance, you welcome the natural flow of life and allow the resistance to be set free."

Your True Nature is Worth Every Ounce of Effort

Energy and enthusiasm are vital to make the radical changes needed to live as one with life. Faithfully staying tuned in to the sound may require effort at times because it is extremely easy to slip back to the old patterns. However, with contagious energy and enthusiasm, living your freedom is guaranteed. It depends purely on what you want for your life. Making the effort to live this freedom is worth every ounce of sweat that you put into it!

Usually, change is only seen in retrospect. It quietly sneaks in the *back door* without you being aware of it. The one that looks for change or progress is the personal identification and it is the personality package that always tries to take ownership of the changes. Looking for results actually stops results from happening or at the very least, can cause difficulties to arise. When you tune in and relax, however, the magic of creation works behind the scenes and your life will transform quite naturally.

Therefore, for the simple and true way forward through life, tune in to the sound. Use the sound and the time spent in the thirty-minute lie-down sessions to step outside your personality identification and sink deeply beneath the arising experiences. This allows you to see and feel any energy that has been trapped in your system throughout the day, as it is. It releases the energy from your hold and gives space for it to disintegrate, simply by you staying out of the flow of the arising experiences.

From this uninvolved and impersonal perspective, you are able to see the creations for the emptiness that they are. Again, you are not judging. You are simply seeing and feeling the truth behind the lies.

This allows the natural order to come into balance and settle back into place. You will also see, from this impersonal perspective, that you bring much more true love and support to people whom you come into contact with, when you aren't emotionally involved in any outcomes.

"The flow of life only becomes blocked when you listen to the
thinking mind and act on its advice."

Shelter from the Storms of Life

Tuning in to the still-point of the sound is like staying in the shelter of the
eye of the storm of life and letting the storm pass by without being touched
by it. You are simply staying as one with your heart instead of getting caught
in the storm.

Staying tuned in to the sound and re-aligning your attention to your true
nature thoroughly rubs against your personality identification. Seeing and
feeling this friction is an important part of staying tuned in to the sound, at
the start.

At times, tuning in will rub the thinking mind raw. This rubbing against
your old motion through life can generate a storm of arising experiences,
both within your system and reflected out in your life. Through these
experiences, you will graphically see how the thinking mind works to disrupt
your relationship with your heart. When you see this, it enables you to break
old patterns of behaviour as you stay tuned in.

The thinking may tell you to feel justified and righteous at these raw times
and spit out blame at others. However, projecting blame is the worst thing
you can possibly do. No one else is ever to be blamed for your feelings or
reactions. Listening to the thinking mind and identifying with your
personality are always the main culprits for any arising difficulties. Acting
out blame in this manner only reinforces the belief in the thoughts, which
makes them build up as previously described.

The greatest opportunities for growth and maturity arise at these raw
moments because you will graphically see and feel the mind's influence.
Therefore, you tune in to the sound and hold the tongue at all costs. Walk
away from a situation for a short period, if you need to, until you are simply
at rest here in this moment again. You are not holding back any emotions;
you are simply feeling them and deeply seeing through the false appearances
of life. You will then welcome any feelings and emotions that mind
identification creates, as you see that every appearance is showing you a
reflection of the one lesson.

"At times, tuning in will rub the thinking mind raw. This rubbing
against your old motion through life can generate a storm of
arising experiences, both within your system and reflected out in
your life."

Just in case it hasn't been mentioned enough, this lesson is that you are already the one powerful peace that rests beneath the reflections of life and you can relax and live as this 'one' right now.

As you welcome the feelings and emotions, the cycles of the thinking mind are free to pass. When you stay with the sound, it allows the arising experiences of life to flow without any interference caused by you holding onto these experiences, naming them or accepting them to be true. As you stay tuned in to the unmoving eye of the storms of life, the arising experiences are seen for the empty nonsense that they are. They are drawn into the storm's eye and vanish before they touch you.

"No one else is ever to be blamed for your feelings or reactions. Listening to the thinking mind and identifying with your personality are always the main culprits in any arising difficulties."

Softening into Your True Nature

When you stay tuned in to the sound a real softening will take place in the core of your being. As you give up the fight with life, the harshness that has built up in your personality will disappear.

In a very short time, your friends and family will notice that you have changed on a deep level. They will be amazed by your new-found confidence and happiness. Often, you won't notice these changes because you are not focused on, or interested in, the details of the change. Your focus is on your beautiful heart!

The mind and body may become restless as these deep realisations settle into normality. This restlessness is a wonderful sign that things are on the move.

Do your best to bless every situation and every feeling. Know that each situation and person in your life is perfect and that they are here for your benefit, to bring you closer to your true nature. Know also that any discomfort will pass as you continue to remain tuned in.

Don't make any life-changing decisions during times of agitation. With such upheaval, it would be so easy to drop the responsibilities of life and simply walk away. But the question arises, 'Where to go?' There is only *this* moment, so take life one moment and one step at a time, until these changes settle. Also, stay tuned in to the sound.

"The greatest opportunities for growth and maturity arise at these raw moments because you will graphically see and feel the mind's influence. Therefore, you tune in to the sound and hold the tongue at all costs."

Profound Silence

In day-to-day living, when you are at rest here with the sound, a profound silence comes into your life. This is not a physical silence, but a deep silence of your spirit. The sound anchors your will-power to your heart and with consistency, the motion of your true nature takes over, leaving you in peace.

As you fall in love with bonding to your heart, you will stay tuned in to the still-point of the sound on a stable basis. This sound is the place that enlivens and feeds your body and quietens the mind, ensuring a swift and easy transition back to living as one with your heart. Then, you are fully open and ready to receive the infinite love that your heart has for you. You will find that the more you are willing, the more you will receive.

"Do your best to bless every situation and every feeling. Know that each situation and person in your life is perfect and that they are here for your benefit, to bring you closer to your true nature."

What You Have Learnt from Chapter Twelve

You can stop creating the thinking mind because the thinking mind doesn't exist without you. Instead, you can use the 'oneness' of your heart as your compass to draw you home to the truth.

Keep in close 'feeling' contact with your heart and in gratitude. Simply say a silent *'Thank you'* for the endless beauty of life and listen to your heart's guidance.

When you set an internal declaration of high spiritual truth, you challenge the old beliefs that are in the unconscious mind. The false is revealed to be seen, felt and allowed to be naturally set free from being held in your system.

The appearance of conflict provides the opportunity for growth. It ultimately strengthens the bond with your heart. These conflicts are inevitable because they are already trapped in your system and they need to be set free.

Renew your gratitude and this will bring you back on course, as you tune in to the sound and rest in the power of peace.

It is never too late to tune in to the still-point of the sound. 'Now' is always the perfect time to tune in again and you are free, standing in your one true essence.

In welcoming any resistance, you welcome the natural flow of life and allow the resistance to be set free.

The flow of life only becomes blocked when you listen to the thinking mind and act on its advice.

At times, tuning in will rub the thinking mind raw. This rubbing against your old motion through life can generate a storm of arising experiences, both within your system and reflected out in your life.

No one else is ever to be blamed for your feelings or reactions. Listening to the thinking mind and identifying with your personality are always the main culprits in any arising difficulties.

The greatest opportunities for growth and maturity arise at these raw moments because you will graphically see and feel the mind's influence. Therefore, you tune in to the sound and hold the tongue at all costs.

Do your best to bless every situation and every feeling. Know that each situation and person in your life is perfect and that they are here for your benefit, to bring you closer to your true nature.

Chapter Thirteen

Stay in this Eternal Moment of Now and Be Free

∂

This final chapter again encourages profound acceptance of things just as they are. You also have the opportunity to strongly set your intention to live as this 'one.' In this chapter we will cover:

- Projecting a Future From Your Past

- The Simplicity and Relaxation of Staying Right Here

- Re-Tune the Instrument

- Effortless Peace

- For Your Heart Only

- Let It Be, Just as It Is

- A New Life of Love

- Settle in to Peace

- Have Another Look

- Already Within You

- Focused Intent

- Set a Clear and Final Intention to Live as One with Your Heart

- A Wise Choice

This chapter sets out to wrap everything up for you in as much as it can be wrapped up. So let's make a start. Begin by tuning in and focusing all your attention fully as you read. Settle into the peace and freedom of this, as your true nature.

Projecting a Future From Your Past

Living in the future and projecting what may be ahead for you makes change seem hard. These false ideas project thoughts and lies (worry) onto the future and are an old trick of the thinking mind. They are also a total waste of your attention because they are not true. These thoughts distract your attention, create stress in your body and the joy of this moment is totally ignored and forgotten.

When you are not tuned in to this moment (through hearing the sound), time appears to move faster and nothing seems to really change. You are left waiting in a kind of holding pattern. Like an airplane that is unable to land, you just travel round in the same circles over and over again. You may be able to see the landing strip in the distance, but you can't touch down and land on it. You also can't get out of the plane and lay on the warm grass with the sun gently kissing your skin. When you continue to do the same thing, you get the same results!

Over time, your petrol begins to run out and this feeling of waiting for something that never comes creates stress, anxiety, anger, depression, shame, blame, entrapment and seemingly sudden old age. This sudden old age is because when you do finally look up from this cycle of distraction, years may have passed and you wonder where your life went.

When you listen to any false future projections, they create a sensation of fear in your body. This fear sensation can have you believing you are lost, not good enough, not courageous enough, on the brink of insanity or anything else in between. Don't become caught in believing any of these false ideas. They will keep you stuck, moving round in circles until death comes to your body.

Faith is the cure for getting caught up in this wasted worry. Fear only arises when the mind can't see the path ahead. Faith sees the path clearly and is grateful for it. When you tune in to the sound and melt into peace, you are consciously bringing your full attention into the only moment that exists—this moment right now, with no personal identification.

In this moment, projecting forward or backward is impossible. From here, you will sink deeply into the sound and allow the arising experiences of life to just be as they are, without dragging them into a perceived past or future scenario.

"There is only *this* moment, so take life one moment and one step at a time, until these changes settle. Also, stay tuned in to the sound."

The Simplicity and Relaxation of Staying Right Here

Stay in this moment and don't look forward to, or predict, the experience of the next thing. Remain centred on the flavour of what you have in your life right now, by staying tuned in to your true nature. This is the simplicity of living as this 'one.'

When you are tuned in, the mind is free to think clearly and right decisions are made quickly and easily. You will begin to instinctively know and feel what is right for you, in this moment, without hesitation. Trust your heart to guide you.

As with every aspect of life, don't fix your attention on the act of living, creation or giving. Instead, fix it on the taste of life by tuning in to the sound. When you live from this place, you feel and enjoy the banquet of life right through to the core of your being. You love all of life! You see the abundant joy of life. You feel and give gratitude for these riches. Know that these riches are coming to you as fast as you can receive and use them. Only you have the power to restrict the flow. This flow of riches is opened by you tuning in and surrendering to your heart.

Don't let anything that the mind may conjure up worry you. If you lie awake at night, tune in to the sound. You can tune in to the sound at any time throughout the day. Live with thankfulness that the abundant heart is already yours.

> ## FEEL
>
> Tune in, breathe and feel perfectly confident that you will stabilise as the powerful peace that you are in due time; and you will.

The whole of life wants to support, nurture and love you. Your part of the bargain is to relax and let it!

When you are simply tuned in to this sound, right here in this eternal 'now' moment, no problem exists, ever, and you can simply relax. This fact will be clearly seen when you stay tuned in to this one place of true love. As you stay here, trust in your true nature grows. Instead of trusting any old ideas, the balance of trust tips over and relaxes into the powerful peace that you truly are.

"Faith is the cure for getting caught up in this wasted worry. Fear only arises when the mind can't see the path ahead. Faith sees the path clearly and is grateful for it."

"As with every aspect of life, don't fix your attention on the act of living, creation or giving. Instead, fix it on the taste of life by tuning in to the sound. When you live from this place, you feel and enjoy the banquet of life right through to the core of your being."

Re-Tune the Instrument

Again, don't allow the thinking mind to wander into past and future ideas. Stop thinking about what you are going to do next, according to what you remember doing before.

Retrain the mind to do your bidding, rather than you being pushed around by every whim that the thinking mind comes up with. The feelings are also a large part of the mind's influence. These too need to be retrained and released. Live with the power of your attention tuned in to this moment; tuned in to the still-point of the sound. From here, you will instinctively know what moves to make and which feelings to trust. Everything will become obvious to you.

Drop the idea of doing things because they are good for your health or simply because of what the thinking mind judges as right. Only do what your heart moves you to do. Then, you will do each of these things because you are moved to do them, out of love for your true nature and its enjoyment, rather than because of any ideas or beliefs of the thinking mind.

IMAGINE

Imagine how much easier life will be without being thrown around by the thinking mind.

Tune in, relax and feel the relief as it flows through your body.

"Live with thankfulness that the abundant heart is already yours. Tune in, breathe and feel perfectly confident that you will stabilise as the powerful peace that you are in due time; and you will."

Effortless Peace

The only effort required to rest as the powerful peace that you are, is in the very first moments of tuning in to the still-point of the sound. Once you are here, anchored in this moment, that is the end of it. Tuning in again is only needed when you find that you have risen back into the trivial activity of personal identification.

Stay tuned in and you are immediately saved. Learn to live from here and life will never be the same. Everything you have ever yearned for is here, now, when you tune in and melt into the joy of your true nature.

When your body feels constricted, in fight with life, or you are trying too hard, come back to simplicity and tune in to the sound. It truly is this straightforward. The good news is that it will get easier with each passing day.

Living as the peace that you are is easy. It simply involves returning back to the sound, in this moment. Then, you step back from the personality package, relax into peace and stop the internal tug-of-war. Set yourself free from the struggle and pain of your personality.

TUNE IN & RELAX

Tune in, relax and simply let your heart just be here; naked, empty, still, nothing.

"The whole of life wants to support, nurture and love you. Your part of the bargain is to relax and let it!"

For Your Heart Only

Your heart is the essence of life; the core of your creation. Everything comes from your heart. There is nothing that it doesn't contain. You, everyone else and all of life flows from the powerful peace that you are.

Your heart is yours and it is everyone else's too. Your heart connects you to creation. It is the essence and the fullness of life. In fact, it is everything that ever was and ever will be.

Either you undertake a lifestyle change for your true nature alone or you are in it for ego gratification. No other possibility exists! If you are in it to build up your personality, perhaps to become a more *spiritual* person, it will never work. This is because the thinking mind will pat your personality on the back and give it credit for the changes. If you believe these thoughts, you are constantly re-building any break-down of personal identification at the same time as it occurs. Understandably, this motion strengthens the personal identification or ego and keeps it alive.

"The only effort required to rest as the powerful peace that you are, is in the very first moments of tuning in to the still-point of the sound. Once you are here, anchored in this moment, that is the end of it."

The moment your personality is truly revealed for what it is, you see that only the one powerful peace that you are is here and true. As a result, the idea of your personality dissolves into thin air.

Resting in the sound is resting in pure peace. This really means peace. There is no particular experience; no feelings, thoughts, reactions, internal world, or gratification. Simply refuse to listen to the thinking mind and allow your true nature to take over. There will be only peace.

"Living as the peace that you are is easy. It simply involves returning back to the sound, in this moment. Then, you step back from the personality package, relax into peace and stop the internal tug-of-war."

Let It Be, Just as It Is

Selflessly, let there be no particular experience, as far as possible. Welcome whatever happens to be here and stay with the sound. This opens the space for magic to take place. This place of peace is who you are. You are just not used to living from this place and therefore, it may take a short period of re-adjustment before you fully appreciate this peace.

You have already made the clear intention to choose to love your heart without condition, rather than relying on warm and fuzzy feelings that will fade. Trust that this love will pull you through even tough times and stick it out.

You are already free from everything. However, it is incredibly easy to have a mental image of freedom and to completely underestimate the true effects of it. It is also extremely easy at this stage, to add a subtle mental creation to the picture. You may add an insight, a feeling of joy, love, bliss, freedom or ecstasy—anything that will objectify this pure peace. This objectification helps the mind to think that it has been worth the effort, gratifying to your personality or your image of *truth*.

Any sense of having attained something, no matter how subtle the experience, is not the pure freedom of the peace that you are. The beauty of your true nature is beyond your highest experiences of love. It is love without subject or object. It just is; one; complete unto itself.

"Set yourself free from the struggle and pain of your personality.
Tune in, relax and simply let your heart just be here; naked,
empty, still, nothing."

A New Life of Love

What are you prepared to give up to live as the beauty and joy of your true nature? To be free from being pushed around by this automatic move of falsity is worth giving up your life for. But if you wish to know what is precisely required, it's giving up your old life. Give it up to your heart and stay with the sound, in this place only.

The deepening of this love affair with your heart will bring commitment to staying tuned in through your daily living. You will begin to accept the human condition, with its unconscious personal identification, in its entirety. You will also allow your personality to be, just as it is. You will no longer identify with it or feed it with your attention and in time, the personality will become softly patient and compassionate.

This acceptance will be reflected to you from your friends, family, co-workers and anyone whom you interact with. They will begin to accept and support you in whatever you do in your life. It cannot be stressed enough that there will never be any regret for the feelings of grief, upset, or discomfort which may occur—not even for a moment. Won't it be great to look back on the effort and see how generously it has paid off?

"Any sense of having attained something, no matter how subtle
the experience, is not the pure freedom of the peace that you are.
The beauty of your true nature is beyond your highest experiences
of love."

Settle in to Peace

Your body needs the appearance of time to get used to this radical change to the core of your perception and being. It also takes time for the built-up residual energies of your personality identification to end. How long this takes is entirely up to you. Whatever you believe, you will create. It *can* be over in a moment. This moment!

No matter how long it takes, don't think of time. Only the thinking mind measures progress because progress automatically implies past and future. Look only at this present moment. It is here that you are truly free and in joy.

In reality, time is false; there is only this one eternal 'now' moment. Your true nature is already here and perfect. It is only the thinking mind that projects this freedom as being out of your reach and into a distant future possibility. This projection is simply not true.

TUNE IN

Tune in to the sound again, in this moment and your life will change forever.

Tune in and you will earn all the freedom that you could ever imagine.

The freedom you receive is in direct proportion to what you give. This is reflected in the moments that you spend being tuned in and living from the 'oneness' of your true nature.

"In reality, time is false; there is only this one eternal 'now' moment. Your true nature is already here and perfect. It is only the thinking mind that projects this freedom as being out of your reach and into a distant future possibility."

Have Another Look

It is strongly recommended that you re-read part of this book once a day for at least the first four weeks. You can read a section or a chapter. However, make sure you read through from the beginning at least three times. Reading out-loud to yourself is also a very powerful way of absorbing the energy of the book. When reading to yourself in this manner, you will read, speak and hear the words. This has the energy coming at you from multiple directions.

Re-reading will allow the essence of this sharing to penetrate and break through the crust of your personality identification. The more you review this book and spend time tuning in, the more you deepen into enjoying the glorious love affair with your beautiful heart After using the book in this way, you can simply open the book on a page and see what life wants to show you.

"The freedom you receive is in direct proportion to what you give. This is reflected in the moments that you spend being tuned in and living from the 'oneness' of your true nature."

Simply tune in to the sound and move from this one powerful place of peace. From here, you will feel the true love of life for yourself. Then, you can re-read this sharing from an experiential perspective. As you grow, each time you read this book you will gain deeper insights that you had missed earlier. These deeper insights clearly show that you are growing up and maturing into living your true nature.

Hearing it said that personal identification isn't true, is easy. Thinking personal identification isn't true, is also easy. However, this personal identification will still feel incredibly real to begin with, as you have known and lived with it for so long.

Only when you are stably re-attuned to your true nature, will you be free from the limitations and the influence of your personality. Therefore, persevere, regardless of what is put in your path and continue to come back to the natural simplicity and joy of your heart.

By staying tuned in as you move, your every move in life will be strong and confident. This brings the full power of your true nature to every moment and to every action in this moment. Your heart will then flow through inspiring every step you take.

If you think that you only need to read this book once, this is purely the thinking mind speaking and the first step you need to take is not to listen to it. You always receive what you give; and in this case, it is a thousand-fold.

FEEL

As you read, feel the words only from your direct experience of being tuned in to your heart. Then, the words will be read straight into the core of your being.

Read like you are reading with the whole matrix of your body's system and soon, you will be living your life in this wholesome manner.

Living the powerful peace that you are is a beautiful and simple change of life. Your heart opens its arms wide and folds you up inside, where you will create a life of joy and freedom, living open-handedly, curled up in the sunlit warmth on the lap of your beloved heart.

"The more you review this book and spend time tuning in, the more you deepen into enjoying the glorious love affair with your beautiful heart."

Already Within You

Your true nature needs nothing; it is already complete, already perfect. It already is. It is that which is. While your body and the mind persist in motion, your heart is in feeling. It has no journey to embark on and no destination to reach. It is where life springs from. Every moment of life is the perfect expression of this 'one.'

The love of your heart is already and always devoted to you, accepting you just as you are. When you turn your attention back to it, you dissolve into the love that your true nature is; the love that is already here. You also stop dwelling on your perceived problems. Instead, you will become aware of what you can do for others through your heart's move, in the full understanding of the 'oneness' of life.

All life comes out of this 'one' and your one point of power is now. When you fix your attention on staying tuned in to the sound, it nourishes the truth and calls it forth into your life with its full force and potential. The strength and creative power in your life is given to you by the faith that you have in yourself; the faith that you have in your true nature.

A life that contains no faith creates no peace and joy because it will constantly be moved to look for this peace from outside of itself, instead of contentedly being this peace now. You will never be given anything true from outside of you because, as you now know, life is only ever a reflection of the truth within.

The more you stay tuned in to the still-point of the sound, the more your faith is built upon by your personal experience. This faith is built upon by you, loving your true nature with all your heart. As you live in this manner, the power of peace is yours. Words are not needed to communicate this peace to others. They will feel this peace in your presence and will be drawn to you because of it.

The way to natural happiness, peace and prosperity (in its fullest sense) is in being in conscious union with your heart. Unifying yourself with this 'one' in unquestioning faith and gratitude guarantees your freedom, ensuring a wonderful life. In truth, there is nothing anyone can teach you. They can only call you to uncover what is already within you.

"The strength and creative power in your life is given to you by the faith that you have in yourself; the faith that you have in your true nature."

All information in this book is only a guide; the choice is yours. This is the joy of the 'oneness' of life. Learn to follow it and let it take you past all limitations to a world of peace, love and harmony. Success is the only possibility, because the one power of creation is all there is. It is the very core of your creation and the wellspring of life.

> "The way to natural happiness, peace and prosperity (in its fullest sense) is in being in conscious union with your heart. Unifying yourself with this 'one' in unquestioning faith and gratitude guarantees your freedom, ensuring a most wonderful life."

Focused Intent

Success in life is all about focus. What you focus your attention on is your God. Consequently, if you have other aspirations that you believe are more important to you, you will never willingly put in the energy and attention that staying tuned in requires. This distracted focus prevents you from stably living your true nature. You cannot hope to live in peace with an internal attitude of war!

Such an attitude will continually drive you away from what you long for—your true heart's desire, which is to consciously live the one reality of life. The intent to live stably as this 'one' that you are begins in the mind and is impossible with a mental attitude that is hostile to it.

The majority of people live their lives without any clear intent. This leads to a dispersal of energy in many different directions and in reality, nothing is achieved. Internal conflict is created and pain and suffering ensue. Your intent and the integrity to stick with that intent fit together like a hand in a glove. They are both crucial to stably living your true nature. Therefore, you will need to single-pointedly fix your attention on what your true intent is and bring your full integrity to it.

This single-pointed focus on staying tuned in to your true nature engages the law of attraction until your natural and unconscious focus of attention is simply held right here. You need the fastest and most direct route to permanently stay in the peace that you are. Tuning in to the still-point of the sound and resting with your heart is a very fast and direct route. From here, you will immediately live in freedom.

> "Your intent and the integrity to stick with that intent fit together like a hand in a glove. They are both crucial to stably living your true nature."

Set A Clear and Final Intention to Live as One with Your Heart

The only intention that will actually bring riches to your door is the intention to live as your true nature; as one with life. Your intention is a very powerful force. Without clear intention, you will not make the commitment to change your life to living from the natural happiness and joy of your true nature.

Life is always here to help you to change. It is here to help you to stop believing the thinking mind, to see the true 'oneness' and to set a final and clear intention to live this 'oneness' in your everyday life. Generally, this help from life takes the form of pain and disaster to push you towards deciding to choose change and to finally learn the 'one' lesson. Pain and disaster are only needed if you ignore or fight with the signs that life shows you. This book is one of those signs.

Listening to the thinking mind causes inner struggle and brings uncertainty and indecision. These are stumbling-blocks for many people. The very moment you truly see (from the natural happiness of your true nature) this one habit of believing the thinking mind and its indecision, you will understand how this fundamental habit limits the confident and happy expression of your life. In this moment of recognition, you will finally realise that the thinking mind and your personality have no power whatsoever!

To overcome this one habit, the simple rule is always to tune in to the peace that you are. Tuning in to the still-point of the sound is a wonderfully simple way of doing just this. Easy isn't it?

This intention to tune in to your true nature is the final intention you ever have to make. For a committed person like you, it will be a breeze! Strictly speaking, there is no choice; there is just the thinking mind's idea that you can choose to live without life. However, until you see this in your own direct experience and live it in your everyday existence, you can use this idea that you have a choice to actively change your internal attitude and create a clear intention.

The truth is that you are destined to live as one with your heart because that is all there is. However, making this intention within you helps you to feel like you have some say in the matter!

"This single-pointed focus on staying tuned in to your true nature engages the law of attraction until your natural and unconscious focus of attention is simply held right here."

The one eternal question is: Will you relax and live your true nature willingly? So, now you have to choose between the struggle of living through the thinking mind or the ease of living your life by staying tuned in to the 'oneness' and peace that you are.

> **FEEL**
>
> Let yourself get in touch with how each of these choices feels to you and set a clear, deep and definite intention within you.
>
> Now!

"The very moment you truly see (from the natural happiness of your true nature) this one habit of believing the thinking mind and its indecision, you will understand how this fundamental habit limits the confident and happy expression of your life."

A Wise Choice

Congratulations! Since you are still here, you have made the choice of wisdom. Now that you have set the clear intention to live with the natural happiness and 'oneness' of your true nature, you will bring more and more peace into your daily life. You will stop paying extra attention to the thinking mind and its battle. In its place, you will nurture your creation (as one with the heart of this creation) and live its beauty and joy.

You will now continue to build a strong and joyous relationship with your heart. Your sense of humour will grow as you live in joy. You will also meet challenges with this fresh humour, taking any conflict in your stride.

This relationship with your heart will open you up to feel the innate love, fearless faith and surrender to the beauty of life, which are always already here in the present of this moment. Now that you have set this final wise intention to give priority to living your true nature, you are invited to re-orient your attention to living the natural happiness of your heart and set down the old burdens created by the thinking mind.

Move forward to learning this easy way to revolutionise your life, where you will begin to live the natural beauty of your true nature in your everyday living. Clear intention does ninety percent of the work. Now all you need to put in is your ten percent and get ready for a miracle!

"You are destined to live as one with your heart because that is all there is."

What You Have Learnt from Chapter Thirteen

There is only *this* moment, so take life one moment and one step at a time, until these changes settle. Also, stay tuned in to the sound.

Faith is the cure for getting caught up in this wasted worry. Fear only arises when the mind can't see the path ahead. Faith sees the path clearly and is grateful for it.

As with every aspect of life, don't fix your attention on the act of living, creation or giving. Instead, fix it on the taste of life by tuning in to the sound. When you live from this place, you feel and enjoy the banquet of life right through to the core of your being.

Live with thankfulness that the abundant heart is already yours. Tune in, breathe and feel perfectly confident that you will stabilise as the powerful peace that you are in due time; and you will.

The whole of life wants to support, nurture and love you. Your part of the bargain is to relax and let it!

The only effort required to rest as the powerful peace that you are, is in the very first moments of tuning in to the still-point of the sound. Once you are here, anchored in this moment, that is the end of it.

Living as the peace that you are is easy. It simply involves returning back to the sound, in this moment. Then, you step back from the personality package, relax into peace and stop the internal tug-of-war.

Set yourself free from the struggle and pain of your personality. Tune in, relax and simply let your heart just be here; naked, empty, still, nothing.

Any sense of having attained something, no matter how subtle the experience, is not the pure freedom of the peace that you are. The beauty of your true nature is beyond your highest experiences of love.

In reality, time is false; there is only this one eternal 'now' moment. Your true nature is already here and perfect. It is only the thinking mind that projects this freedom as being out of your reach and into a distant future possibility.

The freedom you receive is in direct proportion to what you give. This is reflected in the moments that you spend being tuned in and living from the 'oneness' of your true nature.

The more you review this book and spend time tuning in, the more you deepen into enjoying the glorious love affair with your beautiful heart.

The strength and creative power in your life is given to you by the faith that you have in yourself; the faith that you have in your true nature.

This single-pointed focus on staying tuned in to your true nature engages the law of attraction until your natural and unconscious focus of attention is simply held right here.

The very moment you truly see (from the natural happiness of your true nature) this one habit of believing the thinking mind and its indecision, you will understand how this fundamental habit limits the confident and happy expression of your life.

You are destined to live as one with your heart because that is all there is.

Appendix One

Suggestions for Reviewing This Book

This section is not intended as a study guide in the usual sense. These suggestions are made to help you integrate what you learn from this book; not in an intellectual way, but rather in a feeling or experiential way.

As always, we suggest that before you begin to do anything, you tune in and come to being deeply at rest as one with your heart. Instructions to do this are to be found at various points in the book, beginning with *Chapter Three*.

After reading through the entire book at least three times, cover to cover, we suggest using one of these methods or a combination of these, to review it.

The first way is to simply read and re-read the book from start to finish. There is a definite energy flow to the content. Therefore, immersing yourself in this flow of energy at the start ensures that all key points are absorbed. After the first read-through, reading 3 sections each day can be easily scheduled into your routine. Reading out loud has been mentioned before, however it is worth reinforcing. The benefits are three-fold. You read the words, speak them and hear them. This helps the energy of the words to flow directly into your system and will help your understanding to deepen very quickly.

A second way is to use the book with a study-guide-like approach. Take each subject heading, quote or any part of the text that appeals to you and formulate a question or questions from it.

For instance, from the first heading of the first chapter:

Who Are You and What is the Heart?

You can formulate two questions:

Who am I?

What is my heart?

Rather than engage your mind in answering, we suggest that you tune in, come to being deeply at rest and simply sit with the question. Keep redirecting your attention to the sound, irrespective of what is happening. In this way, you will see anything that needs to be seen or you will merely have a restful time, simply being.

A third way is to go to the 'What You've Learnt' reviews at the end of each chapter, which summarises the highlighted quotes from that chapter. Again, begin by tuning in and resting as one with your heart and let each quote simply be here. You are not trying to understand it or do anything else. Any insights will naturally arise as you rest here. Come back to the sound each time you see that you have attached your attention to any particular thought streams, feelings or sensations.

Another way is to review the book by the means described above, but with the boxed sections throughout the book; again, tuning in and simply resting as you do this.

You can review the book by using any of the suggestions above and going through each bit of text or question. There is absolutely no need to rush this, nor is there any particular result to look for.

The main objective is to rest fully as your heart throughout all that you 'do.' This in itself is success.

Appendix Two

Extra Audio Support

Extra audio support has been created to assist you in integrating living your true nature into your life. Below is a list of extra audios and the sections that they would help you with.

Clarification of the Sound – Chapter Three

The *Good Morning Sunshine audio* will assist you in tuning in (as the first thing you do in the morning) and help to break down any old patterns that are picked up during sleep.

Use this audio every day as soon as you wake up. Remember to tune in first and use the audio to deepen into living as one with your heart and to set your intention to live as your true nature throughout the day.

The Still-Point of Your Attention – Chapter Three

Please refer to the *Still-Point support audio* for further clarification of this place.

The Weakening of the Motion Away – Chapter Three

Please refer to the *Deep Tissue Healing audio* to assist you in becoming familiar with being deeply at rest in your body.

There is Only One Relationship - Chapter Four

The *Relationships audio* will also help you to be safely guided into looking at your past relationships for their patterns.

Projecting the Thinking Mind onto Your True Nature – Chapter Five

The *Letting Go audio* provides help with relaxing into the way life truly is right now.

Strengthening the Power Pack of Your Attention – Chapter Five

Please listen to the *Exercising the Mind audio* support to help you here.

The *Powerful Peace Meditation audio* support will also assist you in strengthening the muscle of your attention.

The Body's Unconscious Responses - To Battle or Escape? – Chapter Six

Please listen to the *Understanding and Accepting Fear audio* for further insight into the fear sensation.

Relaxing into the Way Life Is – Chapter Six

The *Goodnight and Sweet Dreams audio* is available to help you relax into deep sleep.

Using Your Everyday Habits to Create New Successful Habits – Chapter Seven

All of the extra audio recordings will help you to integrate this habit of tuning in into the routine of your life. These audio recordings cover:

- Getting up in the morning with *Good Morning Sunshine*
- Brushing your teeth with *Mirror Magic*
- Releasing yourself from *Feeling Stuck*
- *Everyday Activity And Working*
- Going to sleep with *Goodnight And Sweet Dreams*

Lifestyle Transformation and Using Time Wisely – Chapter Seven

The *Everyday Activity and Working audio* is designed to help you to bring tuning in to the sound into your daily life, while busily moving around. Simply have it playing in the background and it will repeatedly remind you to tune in and live from the happiness of your true nature, in the one powerful peace that you truly are.

Permanently Responsible – Chapter Eight

The *Mirror Magic meditation audio* brings love and forgiveness and a deeper understanding of your true nature.

Would You Choose Positive or Negative if You Were in Charge of the Power Supply? – Chapter Eleven

The *Good Morning Sunshine audio* support will also assist you in shaking off any heavy energy patterns that you may be carrying around.

These, and more, extra audios are available from:

http://www.TrueNatureCentre.com/shortcut-to-inner-peace

www.TrueNatureCentre.com

"The world is in your chest and every detail of life has been
created as a reflection of this gently spinning world."

NOTES

NOTES